The modern economy

A theoretical debate and its practical implications

L. W. T. Stafford

Longman
London and New York

Longman Group Limited London and New York

*Associated companies, branches and representatives
throughout the world*

*Published in the United States of America
by Longman Inc., New York*

First published 1976

Library of Congress Cataloging in Publication Data

Stafford, L. W. T.
   The modern economy

   Includes bibliographies.
    1. Economics. 2. Keynesian economics.   I. Title.
HB171.5.S76   330.15'6   75—20322
ISBN 0—582—44357—1
ISBN 0—582—44358—X pbk.

Set in IBM Journal 10 on 12pt
and printed in Great Britain by
Lowe and Brydone (printers) Ltd, Thetford, Norfolk

Contents

Author's preface   vi

Acknowledgements   viii

1 Models and policy   1
1.1 The power of theory   1
1.2 The influence of Keynesian models   2
1.3 The content of the simple Keynesian model   3
1.4 Money in the Keynesian scheme   6
1.5 The classical alternative   8
1.6 The need for a new synthesis   9
     Notes and references   10

2 The market system   11
2.1 The importance of the market concept   11
2.2 The market as servo-mechanism   12
2.3 Information and time in the market system   13
2.4 Other influences working against market equilibrium   17
2.5 Market definition and boundaries   18
2.6 The Cambridge criticism of the neo-classical position   19
     Notes and references   20

3 The aggregate economy   21
3.1 An aggregation of markets   21
3.2 The possibility of equilibrium in the system   22
3.3 Economic equilibrium in the primitive exchange economy   24
3.4 Equilibrium in a money economy   25
3.5 A more complete model   27
3.6 The equilibrating process   28

3.7 Models and economic perspectives 29
Notes and references 29

4 **The new orthodoxy** 30
4.1 The Keynesian pedigree of the standard model 30
4.2 The model formalised 32
4.3 Policy analysis and the attractions of *IS—LM* 32
4.4 A critique of the new orthodoxy 35
4.5 An appraisal of rival orthodoxies 37
Notes and references 39

5 **A revised view of Keynesian economics** 41
5.1 The missing excess demand 41
5.2 Some suggested solutions 42
5.3 The dual-decision hypothesis 44
5.4 The dynamic adjustment process 45
5.5 Keynesian models and the new view 48
5.6 A basis for future work 49
Notes and references 50

6 **Models for disequilibrium analysis** 51
6.1 Some requirements for the analysis 51
6.2 A simple disequilibrium model 52
6.3 Formal presentations of the model 55
6.4 A scenario for the collapse of a classical equilibrium 61
6.5 A simplified method of analysis 63
Notes and references 65

7 **Economic models and the real world** 66
7.1 Economic depression and the plausibility of models 66
7.2 Empirical evidence and the construction of the model 69
7.3 The model and inflation 71
7.4 Non-Keynesian inflation 74
7.5 Understanding and prediction 76
7.6 The acceptance of hypotheses in economic science 77
Notes and references 79

8 **Policy and growth** 80
8.1 The transition to a system in motion 80
8.2 Investment and productivity 81
8.3 The growth path of the economy 83
8.4 Growth and the model 84
8.5 The United Kingdom growth experience 86
8.6 An extension to policy options 87
Notes and references 90

9	**The dynamics of prices and incomes**	91
9.1	The failure of demand management	91
9.2	Productivity and information flows	92
9.3	The circumvention of the labour market	93
9.4	Interaction between economic and social systems	96
9.5	Does inflation matter?	97
	Notes and references	97
10	**Problems of economic control**	98
10.1	The system to be controlled	98
10.2	Concepts in the control of socio-economic systems	99
10.3	The objectives of economic policy	102
10.4	Control and the model	103
10.5	Stability and rigidities in the control of economic systems	107
	Notes and references	109
11	**A final comment**	110
	Appendix I A technical commentary	112
AI.1	Static and dynamic analysis in economics	112
AI.2	The use of simultaneous equation models	114
AI.3	Block diagrams and mathematical analysis	116
AI.4	Equilibrium growth paths	117
	References	119
	Appendix II Selected statistics of the UK economy	120
	Index	121

Author's preface

Economists are criticised by laymen for the enclosed and obscure nature of their debate, for their impenetrable jargon and for their inability to reach generally agreed conclusions. A lack of unanimity is a necessary part of the process by which any science advances, but because the subject matter of economics is so closely related to everyday activities on the one hand and to affairs of high policy on the other disagreement amongst economists is considered to be perverse and reprehensible. It is inevitable, too, that the academic and technical discussion should become entangled with the parallel political debate. One way of avoiding the problems which this involvement brings is to retreat into the apparent neutrality of mathematical abstraction but although this has brought benefits in the way of improved techniques of analysis and a much tighter logic, it excludes many behavioural and social factors which are seen, increasingly, to be significant. It is necessary to recognise the validity of both the academic and the political debates and to acknowledge that they are not separate from each other but have evolved together. This close relationship between theoretical analysis and issues of policy gives rise to a quite pressing need to present students and interested laymen with a review and formalisation of the current discussion, so that the debate becomes accessible and can give perspective to observed social and economic trends.

It is not possible to do justice to the modern discussion, nor to give its flavour, without making any reference at all to the underlying mathematics, but technicalities have been kept to a minimum and where mathematics have obtruded into the text they have been set out in their simplest form. In most chapters the discussion is verbal and diagrammatic and where some additional technical explanation is required it has been given separately in Appendix I. Even here there is little to daunt even the faintest mathematical heart.

Finally, the view has been taken that the purpose of economic analysis is to gain an understanding of the world. The furtherance of ambition or the confounding of opponents may occasionally have been dominant motives for the protagonists in economic as in other academic debates, but this is not our concern. The coverage of the arguments is not, therefore, exhaustive. The intention has been to provide an opportunity for readers to enter into the discussion and to use the tools of analysis which are so acquired to attempt to form a consistent and rational view of that part of human experience with which macro-economics is concerned.

Acknowledgements

We are indebted to the following for permission to reproduce copyright material:
The author and *The Times* for a letter by Mr Neild to *The Times* on 26 February 1974. We are grateful to Macmillan for permission to reproduce the diagrams on pp. 116–17 from *Mathematical Economics* by R. G. D. Allen, 1965.

1
Models and policy

1.1 The power of theory

Economic policies have their roots in social and economic theory. Often the particular theories which influence politicians and administrators have been refuted or discredited by serious thinkers in the fields concerned, but the power of ideas continues even when their logic has been shown to be false. This view of the power of ideas is quite at variance with the widely held notion that theory, and especially economic theory, is arid and quite unrelated to the practicalities of the 'real world'. The force which economic theory exercises in the world of affairs is due to two things: firstly to man's need to have a coherent vision of events as an ordered rather than as a random sequence and, secondly, to his inability to achieve this without some sort of 'model'.

A model could be defined as a set of concepts and a specification of the relationships between them. In economic analysis, these concepts would be categories of economic agents, such as firms, consumers, workers or government or they could be the quantities which indicated how these agents were performing. These quantities would be profits, wages, consumption expenditures and so on. The relationships might be technical ones, such as that between total output and the number of workers in employment or they might be more loosely specified, behavioural relationships like those which determine the reactions of workers to management policy. Often they will be behavioural relationships quantitatively specified. An example would be that between consumers' expenditure and the level of income. Although economic models may take many forms, it is important to understand that whenever economic discussion takes place, models are being employed. This is so whether the discussion is at a policy making level or at the less momentous, although not necessarily less intense, level of the saloon bar or commuter train. All perceptions of the world depend on the possession of a set of concepts and of ideas about the relationships between them. When the models are incorrect or inappropriate, they give rise to false perceptions of the world. At the governmental level, these perceptions are demonstrated to be false when the policies derived from them are ineffective or harmful. The acceptance of grossly incorrect or excessively simple models by the public at large is likely to lead to misunderstanding of policy, especially when the benefits lie in the fairly distant future. In extreme cases, the general acceptance of crude models can lead to hysterical or aggressive reactions to essentially reasonable policies.

1.2 The influence of Keynesian models

The establishment of effective and workmanlike economic models is, then, not just an academic exercise but is essential for the determination of policy and an important part of education for democracy. Without doubt, the most influential figure in revising the models which guided and informed both policy makers and significant sections of the public in the recent past was John Maynard Keynes. Keynes was very alert to the power of economic ideas and in a well known passage he wrote that 'practical men who believe themselves quite exempt from any intellectual influences are usually the slaves of some defunct economist'. There was an implication that the influence of the defunct economist was unlikely to be benign. Today it is Keynes's own ideas that influence practical men in government and he is twenty-five years dead. Perhaps it is time to ask whether his influence is still benign. During the Second World War and in the early post-war years there seems little doubt that Keynesian ideas were extremely beneficial. Governments learned that it was possible to regulate the level of demand in the economy and acquired the will to do so. They recognised the connexion between total demand and the level of employment and assumed a commitment to avoid high levels of unemployment. Since the models which are used by policy makers are not declared openly and because the policy makers themselves may not be wholly aware of the influences which determine their actions, it is difficult to be precise, but it seems true to say that the dominant model in the early post-war years was a rather simplified Keynesian one. At first, as part of the Keynesian scheme, it seemed to involve a relationship between the rate of interest and the level of economic activity, as instanced by the low interest rate policies of the first post-war Labour Government. Later on, the influence of interest rates was regarded as comparatively unimportant and the regulation of aggregate demand by direct action on government expenditure and taxation became the main aspect of policy. Even after Bank Rate was reactivated in 1951, it was used as a corrective to external currency flows rather than as a regulator of the economy internally. This attitude to the role of interest rates reflects closely the developments in the thinking of academic economists and is still relevant to present day differences of approach. In Keynes's *General Theory*, interest rates do have an effect on the level of investment and, investment being one of the most important, if not the most important, components of total expenditure in the economy, on aggregate demand. Various investigations, and in particular a series of surveys carried out by the 'Oxford Economists' just before the war, had seemed to indicate that businessmen paid little regard to interest rate changes when making their decisions to invest in new capital equipment. This unresponsiveness, or inelasticity, of real as distinct from financial, investment to interest rate changes soon became part of the conventional wisdom and was reflected in the policies of successive governments during the 1950s and 1960s. Once policy makers believed that they could manipulate interest rates without having too serious an effect on the performance of the economy itself, interest rate policy could be used freely to attract funds to Britain whenever an adverse trading position was endangering the pound sterling. Belief in the interest-inelasticity of investment was also one factor in encouraging a cavalier attitude towards monetary policy, so that it was often subservient to the needs of government finance. The confidence that investment was not much influenced by interest rates confirmed the supremacy of Keynesian economics over its rivals, since the effect of interest rates on saving and investment was an essential link in the chain of marked responses required by the 'neo-classical' system which the power of the Keynesian analysis and, it should be said, the force of Keynes's and his followers', polemics had temporarily defeated. The simpler, 'new monetarist' view, which stressed a direct link between the money supply and the level of income, had yet to become a serious contender, at least on the British scene.

The Keynesian view of the economic system dominated the thinking of most British and American policy makers for almost twenty years, but the market view of the economy was defeated only on a macro-economic scale. So far as individual industries or the markets for particular commodities were concerned, the belief, however mistaken, in the effectiveness of the competitive market system continued. This, too, was necessary for it was quite fundamental to the Keynesian approach that control of the economy could be exercised by the manipulation of the economic aggregates, not by tinkering with the detailed working of the subordinate parts of the economy.

1.3 The content of the simple Keynesian model
Before examining the current criticisms of an approach to economic

analysis as powerful and authoritative as that of Keynes, it would be well to attempt a summary of its content from a modern standpoint. The *General Theory of Employment, Interest and Money* was an extremely subtle work and reflected a knowledge and insight into the worlds of finance, business and affairs that was not always so apparent in the work of Keynes's disciples and followers. Both Keynes's own models and those of modern economists who derive their thinking from him have as a fundamental component the idea that there are major sectors of expenditure which depend almost entirely on the level of national income. By far the most important of these is consumption. These expenditures contrast with others which are determined by autonomous influences such as business confidence, the 'animal spirits' of entrepreneurs in Keynes's phrase. The total of all expenditures will be equal to the total of all the incomes of the suppliers of 'factor services', whether these services are those of labour or of entrepreneurs and owners of capital. Saving is then that part of aggregate income, the total of all individual incomes, which people decide not to spend on consumption; in Keynes's words, again, it becomes 'a mere residual'. It is clear that in this little model, which although very simple embodies the essentials of the Keynesian view, decisions to make the independent, that is non-income determined, expenditures are dominant in establishing the level of national income. The most important of these autonomous expenditures are investment, meaning, as usual in this area of discussion, expenditure on new physical assets, and government spending. A schematic diagram would show the system as in Fig. 1.1.

Here I = Investment
G = Government Expenditure, $G_{net} = G - T$
Y = Income
C = Consumption
T = Taxation

The independent expenditures are distinguished from the other elements of the system by their double-lined boxes. The symbol f shows that Consumption (C) depends on (is a function of) income.[1]* It can be seen that there are three components of income in this simple model of which one is in its turn determined by income. It is the 'feedback' from consumption to income that determines how increases in I and G are 'amplified' through the economic system. If the system is set out in the form of two simple equations we have:

$$Y = I + G_{net} + C \tag{1.1}$$

(Income = investment expenditure + government expenditure + consumption expenditure)

* These references apply to the Notes positioned at the end of chapters.

Fig. 1.1   A simple Keynesian model

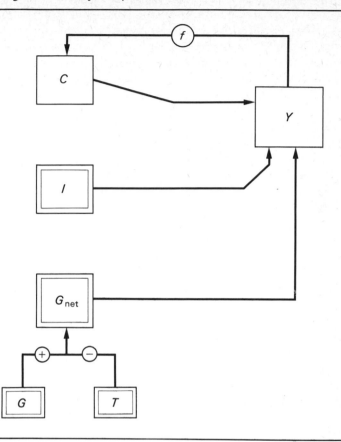

$$C = cY \hspace{8cm} [1.2]$$

(Consumption = a given proportion (c) of income).

The dependency on income shown in [1.2] is the simplest that will conform to Keynes's 'fundamental psychological law' that 'men are disposed, as a rule and on the average, to increase their consumption as their income increases, but not by as much as the increase in income'. It follows from the 'fundamental law' that c will be greater than zero but less than unity. Some very elementary manipulation of the equations gives:

$$Y = \frac{1}{1-c} (I + G_{\text{net}}) \hspace{6cm} [1.3]$$

The coefficient $1/(1-c)$ is the famous 'multiplier', which Keynes thought might, in practice, have a value of about two, indicating that an autonomous increase in investment or government expenditure should give rise to an increase in income of about double that amount. Since the volume of employment could reasonably be taken to depend on the level of income the indication for policy was clear. The same simple model also contains a devastating implicit criticism of the classical scheme which provided the governments of the 1930s with their economic philosophy, for there is nothing in [1.3] which suggests that the eventual level of income will be exactly that which would provide full employment.

Keynes's own exposition of his position in the *General Theory* is more complex but the mechanism for the determination of income and employment is essentially that which is outlined above. The form in which the argument was originally cast was determined by Keynes's own training as a Cambridge economist, by the nature of the conventional thinking which he had to sweep aside and by the problems of his time.

1.4 Money in the Keynesian scheme

To elaborate the model, and to be true to Keynes's thought, a monetary component must be added. This part of the Keynesian model is extremely important since it is here that a central difference between Keynes and his opponents lay nearly forty years ago and persists between their academic descendants today. The link between the level of income, or in an alternative terminology, the level of aggregate demand and the monetary sector is through the effect of the rate of interest on the level of investment. Unlike some of his immediate followers, Keynes did not break the link by insisting on the interest-inelasticity of investment, but supposed that the volume of investment would be likely to vary with the rate of interest. The rate of interest itself may be regarded as being determined by an interaction between the demand for money, depending on both income and the state of expectations, and the money supply. It is this system, now quite complex and with its various elements closely interlinked, that has formed the basis of most of the post-Keynesian developments. The monetary sector is shown in the upper section of Fig. 1.2, where M_{D1} is that part of the demand for money which depends on income and M_{D2} is the part which is influenced by financial expectations. M_S represents the money supply and this is a quantity which is taken as being under the control of the authorities. The symbols E_1 and E_2 show the influence of expectations on the demands for investment goods and for money respectively. With the simple model of Fig. 1.1 added to the monetary component, Fig. 1.2 shows the whole system at this level of elaboration. The direction of causation is shown by the arrows, as before and the symbols enclosed in circles indicate a functional relationship more complex than the mere addition which is to

Fig. 1.2   The Keynesian model with a monetary component

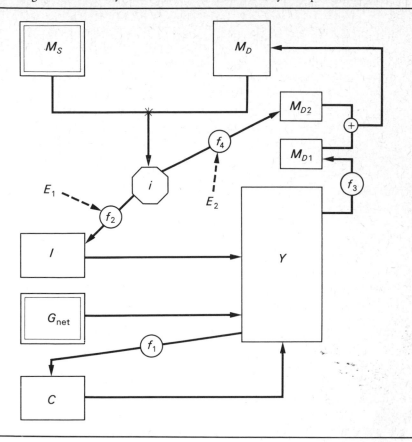

be assumed where uninterrupted arrows are used. The broken lines indicate an influence of a less well-defined kind. It can be seen, by tracing out the path from income through the effect on the demand for money and so on the rate of interest, that investment is no longer independent of the level of income, but has become part of an interacting system. Only the money supply (M_S), government expenditure (G) and the two expectational factors are capable of being independently determined and it is upon these that policy must work. In the hands of some of Keynes's successors, the model illustrated above became distorted so that manipulation of the money supply came to be regarded by many people as an ineffective policy option, leaving government expenditure as the only component which could be varied in order to influence the level of income. Naturally, the G-component in the diagram stands for the net effect of a complicated system of taxes, transfers and expenditures on goods and services. Nevertheless the rejection of the monetary component as an instrument of economic control seriously restricts the range of policy options open to the authorities. Fortunately this rejection was never total and monetary policy remained in the armoury even if distrust of it meant that policy was less effective than it might have been at various times. Less fortunately, the resurgence of the monetary view, effectively from the autumn of 1969, when an IMF delegation virtually dictated policy to a desperate Labour chancellor, seemed to be accompanied by a loss of faith in the appropriateness of other forms of control.[2] This lack of balance followed, very directly, from the acceptance by powerfully placed intellectuals and administrators of the 'new quantity theory' which is discussed later in this book. This influence, in turn, has been swept aside as events have demonstrated its inadequacies.

1.5 The classical alternative

It is convenient to call the traditional analysis, which Keynes sought, quite consciously, to destroy, the 'Classical' view. Both Keynes's predecessors and his early critics were totally loyal to this view and saw employment as being determined by conditions of demand and supply in the labour market. In a properly functioning market, the interaction between the demand for labour and the quantity of labour offering itself for employment at the going wage rate ought to produce tendencies towards an equilibrium level of wages. At this equilibrium wage level, all workers who wished to offer their services would find, without great difficulty, an employer who would wish to give them a job. Some 'frictional' unemployment might exist, but if there was major unemployment, it would be because the general wage level was too high. The level of output was seen as determined by the quantities of the factors of production employed, and in particular by the amount of labour in employment. An excess of total production over the total of goods and services demanded would result in a fall in prices, so that the quantities produced were sold. Changes in the price level would affect the *real* value of wages, but the labour market itself would be concerned with real values and so the economy would come to a full employment equilibrium by means of the interplay between wage and price levels.

The essence of the classical position is as described above, but like the Keynesian model, it requires a monetary sector in order to be complete. Two links are required, one to make the connexion between the quantity of money and the price level and the other to provide a reconciliation between the level of saving and that of investment. These links are not difficult to provide and both depend, as might be expected, on market relationships. The first market link is between the demand for money and the money supply. Given a level of real income determined in the way already described, this relationship should indicate a general level of prices, provided that the velocity of circulation of money is fairly constant. The other relationship is that between the demand for funds for investment and the supply of such funds generated by the community's willingness to save. The level of saving as well as the demand for funds for investment are taken to vary with the rate of interest, which is determined as an equilibrium 'price' by this market. Allowing, reasonably, the saving function to shift with the level of income, completes the system of linkages. Since real income (Y in the Keynesian diagram) and price are determined by market forces, the scope for artificial regulation is limited. Saving and investment are seen as being determined by market forces. In determining income and saving, consumption is also determined. The balance between government expenditure and taxation can only influence the division of income between the government and the private sector but will not change the level of income unless real wages are changed or unless business expectations improve. The only other areas on which policy can be exercised in a classical system are the 'production function', linking the volume of employment to the level of output, and the money supply.

These characteristics of the classicial model were reflected in pre-war economic policy. Throughout the 1920s and 1930s there were repeated denials that government expenditure on public works could do anything other than reallocate outlays, possibly reducing investment in the private sector. There was pressure, sometimes successful, for lower wages and exhortations to work more diligently. These policies now seem to have been brutally inappropriate and were so, but the system which led to their adoption did not have the crude faults in logic which some Keynesians have ascribed to it. It was the logical consistency of the classical model which enabled both academics and civil servants to hold on to it in the face of tragic evidence that it was no longer appropriate.

1.6 The need for a new synthesis
It is suggested that the economic analysis which underlies policy making requires four types of model:

1. A model of the economy, the key model.
2. A market model, for the analysis of factors influencing quantities bought and sold and the prices at which trading is likely to take place.
3. A dynamic model, however crude, for the prediction of growth rates and for the analysis and detection of constraints upon growth.
4. An external trade model, which may be very simple but which should indicate the pressures and constraints imposed by the world economy.

The survey of the macro-economic models which have influenced policy has indicated a high degree of disarray so far as the first and most important type of model is concerned. One current escape from the tensions imposed by the erosion of the fundamental Keynesian models is to substitute computability for conviction, but there is a need for a fresh approach, some new synthesis which will produce a macro-economic model which will explain events and offer hope of a more accurate and sensitive control. When the validity of an intellectual scheme is in doubt, and when it no longer gives the policy insights that events demand, there is a rather desperate willingness to accept a new approach. It was in this climate that the new monetary view was received, and the simplicity of that analysis took it directly into the policy field. The reappraisal of the Keynesian analysis that followed from the work of Clower[3] and Leijonhufvud[4] has had little impact on official thinking because it has not led to an elegant and understandable rearrangement of the concepts held by the policy makers. It is now possible, however, with the help of these recent revisions to see how the Keynesian, classical and monetarist models relate to each other. The establishment of a new synthesis is not easy and cannot concern itself only with broad movements of the major variables; it must begin with a critical analysis of the market process upon which Western economics depends so heavily.

Notes and references

1. For the sake of clarity, consumption is shown here and elsewhere as depending on income. It may be more familiar for some readers to consider consumption as a function of *disposable income* Y_d so that

$$Y_d = Y - T$$

and

$$C = cY_d$$

This formulation gives rise to the famous 'balanced budget' multiplier.

2. This was the occasion when an upper limit to the United Kingdom's Domestic Credit Expansion, the chosen monetary measure, was accepted. See the *Bank of England Quarterly Bulletin*, No. 4, 1969.

3. R. W. Clower, 'The Keynesian counter-revolution: a theoretical appraisal', in *The Theory of Interest Rates*, eds Hahn and Brechling, Macmillan, 1965.

4. A. Leijonhufvud, *On Keynesian Economics and the Economics of Keynes*, Oxford University Press, 1968.

2
The market system

2.1 The importance of the market concept

If the selection of economic policies is dominated by the acceptance of particular models of the economy, as the previous chapter suggested, then the choice of models is likely to depend on whether or not the market system is believed to be effective. 'Effectiveness', here, would mean efficient in securing a response to changing patterns of demand. Those who have confidence in the market system would therefore expect to see the market economy react quickly to changes in consumers' tastes, producing new goods and services as they were required and, almost as quickly, reducing production of commodities that had lost popularity. They would also expect that such an economy, in which energetic and thrustful businessmen could be expected to play a significant and perhaps decisive part, would respond with promptness to anticipated changes in future demand, so that optimistic trading prospects would lead to investment outlays and plans for expansion. Naturally, such a readiness to respond to changing conditions will sometimes lead to reductions in investment expenditures but the market economy's entrepreneurial drive should be sufficient to make these failures of business confidence comparatively rare. The greatest difference between the modern defender of the market system and of his predecessor of, say, fifty years ago would be that today's man would lack the easy optimism of earlier times; he would not be surprised at occasional crises of business confidence and would expect government to intervene at such times; but he would consider that such intervention would best be indirect and limited to the minimum that would restore full employment and an acceptable rate of growth.

Critics of the market system would not believe that such mild intervention would be effective. They would doubt whether the restorative tendencies of the system would be sufficient or even whether they would be present at all. At the most extreme view, this would lead to calls for the replacement of the market system by a 'command economy', in which allocation of resources and the level of activity were determined administratively. For most critics of the market system, however, there would be particular defects which would need strong intervention if they were to be remedied. These defects might concern the way in which the market system distributed the national product amongst the various factors of production and political parties in many Western countries have derived their strength from the need to correct gross inequalities of wealth and income. Perhaps more serious from the point of view of the regulation and control of the economy would be the failure of the market system to generate tendencies towards the establishment of set of equilibrium prices. It is on the existence of such equilibrating tendencies that the claim of the market to be either an efficient or an equitable system rests.

Equilibrating tendencies in the economy as a whole will depend on there being similar tendencies in the individual markets of which the economy is composed. Failures to establish a set of equilibrium prices may follow from imperfections in particular markets, from interactions between markets which, alone, would have reached equilibrium or from discontinuities between major sectors of the economy, so that market forces are prevented from doing their work.

2.2 The market as servo-mechanism

The concept of the self-regulating market is at the heart of all neo-classical models of the economy. Possibly the notion of the market, reacting automatically to correct disturbances, seems archaic and more in keeping with eighteenth- and nineteenth-century ideas than with the macro-economics of the present day. The accepted view, at least in Britain, for many years was that Keynes had finally shown that the 'Classical' economists had nothing of relevance or interest to say about the level of employment and economic activity 'the postulates of the classical theory are applicable to a special case only . . . . Moreover, the characteristics assumed by the classical theory happen not to be those of the economic society in which we actually live, with the result that its teaching is misleading and disastrous if we attempt to apply it to the facts of experience'. For Keynes, the classical economists extended from Adam Smith and Ricardo, through J. S. Mill to Marshall and Pigou. All of these economists shared, as do their modern counterparts, the view of the market as a self-regulating system. So far from being an antique and dangerous folly, it is now suggested that this view is quite in line with modern thought and that such a system would correspond exactly to the 'servo-controlled' systems which play such an important part in automated production lines and the landing of satellites and spacecraft. The essence of such systems is that deviations from target values of a key quantity constitute a 'feedback' of information which sets in train some action to correct the deviation. If such tendencies were at work in an economy the administration, and the interference with the lives and activities of ordinary citizens, necessary to control it would be much reduced. Before this view can be accepted, however, it is necessary to consider very carefully whether the market system does embody the 'servo-mechanism' qualities that are claimed for it.

An immediate problem is that there are two target variables; both price and quantity traded may be regarded as having equilibrium values which the market should attain. In the textbooks this is presented as a simple matter with tendencies towards equilibrium responding to excess demand. The actual process by which equilibrium is reached is usually described only in the most general way, but this is not sufficient if the 'market as servo-mechanism' approach is followed. The market system of the elementary textbooks is usually described as in quadrants A and B of Fig. 2.1. The implication here is that *price* is the target variable and that the correcting device is what Leijonhufvud calls a 'Walrasian homeostat' at which errors in price respond to positive or negative excess demand. A very simple consideration of the process shows that there must be a second ('Marshallian') homeostat at work correcting the *quantities* of the commodity offered on the market. This second correction process is shown by the price discrepancy curve in quadrant C. This curve shows the difference between the supply price and the market price. A negative price discrepancy (market price too low) leads to a reduction in the quantity offered on the market, since it implies that individual firms must be operating at outputs too high to give maximum profits. It appears that the two homeostatic devices built in to the market system represents two sets of forces which must be present if equilibrating tendencies are to be produced. These two necessary pressures are: (i) the need to adjust prices in order to sell goods already produced or contracted for; and (ii) the drive to maximise profits. If firms respond slowly to these pressures, or lack information about the urgency of their market situation, then the two correcting devices may work unevenly or with time-lags so that oscillations are produced about the equilibrium values. There may then be either long periods during which prices are out of equilibrium or there may be no tendency towards equilibrium at all.

2.3 Information and time in the market system

The classicists' case will not stand unless tendencies towards market equilibrium exist. Although interactions between markets may disturb

Fig. 2.1 Equilibrating forces in a single market

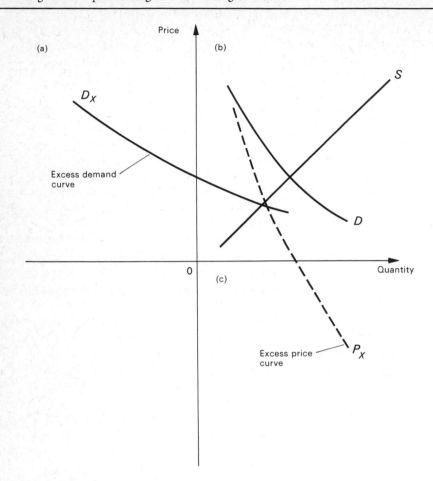

equilibrium, all that is necessary to overturn the neo-classical models is a demonstration that equilibrating pressures are absent or ineffective in single markets. This is by no means easy; all that has been done so far is to show that the tendencies towards equilibrium will not necessarily be effective. To some extent, this is where the matter rests, since obvious failures to reach equilibrium and gross maldistributions of resources may well have been due to interference with the market system or to market imperfections which could be removed. More evidence and a deeper analysis are necessary before a better assessment can be made.

One of the requirements for the effective working of the market system is a full and free flow of information. For the market to operate like the models of the first-year texts, perfect information is needed. From the supply side, as discussed above, the firm would need information about prices charged and quantities unsold by other sellers. Accurate and prompt information would also be needed about costs and profit margins. Even within the firm, such data might well be inaccurate or delayed, so that response to a non-equilibrium might not be immediate.

The situation outlined in the previous section carried the assumption that a stable demand curve existed, but buyers, too, may lack full information. The more that sellers are in disarray, charging slightly different prices from each other and reacting with varying degrees of promptness to changing market conditions, the more information buyers will require in order to make good bargains. If, following Stigler,[1] we assume that buyers and potential buyers are faced with a distribution of prices, and that the probability of finding after a single search, a seller quoting a given price is proportional to the number of sellers quoting that price, then the process by which the equilibrium price is established may be seen as one of inter-action between buyers and sellers in a common situation of imperfect information. Each 'search' will represent a foray into the market and will end when the buyer finds a seller. If the buyer thinks it worthwhile he will carry out a further search in the hope of finding a seller quoting a lower price. At the end of a sequence of searches, the buyer will make his purchase at the lowest price encountered. The number of searches made will depend on the gain expected from another search as compared with the cost of making the additional search; that is search will continue until the expected gain is equal to the marginal cost of search. The extent to which the search for lower prices affects the behaviour of sellers is likely to depend on the cost of search, that is on whether information is expensive or cheap. The initial distribution of prices offered by sellers might be as in Fig. 2.2a: As buyers begin the search process they will tend to ignore high price sellers and the more fortunate ones will tend to cluster around the low price sellers. The sellers offering higher prices, perhaps those in the upper quartile of the distribution, will find their sales falling off and, with a situation of 'localised excess supply' will tend to respond to the Walrasian homeostat and lower their prices. In the lower quartile the sellers will experience localised excess demand and will tend to raise their price. As a result the shape of the distribution will change as shown in Fig. 2.2b. The eventual distribution and the position of the modal price, which may represent an approximation to the theoretical equilibrium price, will depend upon supplies' cost curves as well as upon buyers' search activity. The buyers' desire for a bargain would tend to locate the mode towards the lower end of the central part of the distribution, but the suppliers'

Fig. 2.2   Search and the distribution of prices

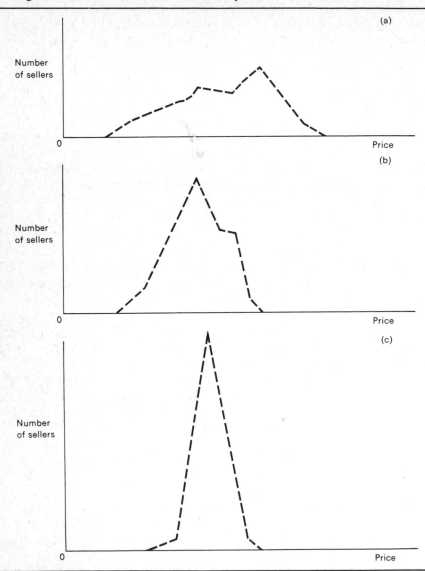

need to make normal profits might tend to locate the mode at a rather higher price. The sequence might be completed with a distribution rather like Fig. 2.2c.

It can be readily accepted that only with perfect information, that is with information available to both buyers and sellers without delay and without cost will a single equilibrium price be established. This, of course, will provide one of the necessary conditions for the familiar perfect market of elementary economics. With less than perfect information, there will be delays in responses to market conditions and there will be, at any one time, a range of prices over which bargains are made. If the range is narrow and is grouped around the true equilibrium price, this may not invalidate the conditions for the effective operation of the market system and the classicists' models may not be inappropriate.

2.4 Other influences working against market equilibrium

Enough has been established to show that even when only one simple market is concerned, equilibrating tendencies cannot be taken for granted. So long as this small doubt remains, a further area of uncertainty is bound to exist; even though most markets within an economy enjoy tendencies towards equilibrium, the existence of a few, or even one, market which fails to reach equilibrium may lead to non-equilibrium prices in other, related markets. If this is likely to happen, faith in the classical market system must be weakened. This rather complex question is best considered in the following chapter, when the consequences of considering the economy as an aggregation of markets are examined, but a preliminary answer might be that all is likely to be well if *income* effects are unimportant.[2] They may be very important indeed.

A less technical objection to continued faith in the market system is that many prices are set not by the actions of numbers of individual buyers and sellers but as part of the marketing policies of very large firms. The importance of the large corporation in the economic life of capitalist countries can hardly be doubted and, as J. K. Galbraith suggested some years ago,[3] it may be that their advantages lie not merely in the economics of large scale production but also in their increased power to plan and control the market situation. At first glance it seems that the classical market system must lie in ruins; prices are set by large firms with monopoly power, high-pressure advertising using the facilities of modern communications media permits the manipulation of demand and, management being separated from ownership, profit maximisation is no longer the principal business motivation.[4] Although there is a persuasive and extensive literature suggesting that all this is so, it may be that something can be salvaged at the macro-economic level if not at the level of the single firm or the single market.

Firstly it should be said that although the literature and the empirical investigations, where they exist, may suggest that profit maximisation is not the dominant motivation which the theoretical models require, they do not in any way indicate that profit does not matter at all. The Marshallian

homeostat may react sluggishly but it is unlikely to be quite out of action.
A further reason for retaining some faith in the market system is that even
the most powerful monopolistic corporation with the most lavish
advertising budgets is not able to determine the pattern of consumer
spending to the extent claimed by Galbraith. Corporate plans do go wrong
and neither the theory of imperfect competition nor plain experience
indicate that monopoly power can be exercised without regard to the
demand functions for the products concerned. Advertising and sales
promotion expenditures may be one of the several independent variables
on the right-hand side of such functions, but it is unlikely in most practical
situations to be a dominant one.

2.5 Market definition and boundaries

The question of whether or not market forces will be effective is closely
connected with the way in which particular markets are defined. It is
perhaps too seldom recognised that the limits which are set on a market for
the purposes of analysis or discussion are conventional rather than natural.
This is so even when the market is highly formalised and these are well-
established market institutions. Where such institutions exist, they usually
improve information flows within the market concerned and so help to
define the limits of the market and to protect the trading within those
limits from the incursions of the outside world. In recent years the
artificiality of the boundaries between formally defined markets has
become increasingly marked. Financiers and businessmen making up and
revising portfolios of assets, both 'real' and financial, will make use of the
institutions provided but they are not likely to be over concerned to stay
within the specialist confines that were once thought to be sacrosanct.

Although there is an element of arbitrariness in the setting of market
boundaries, the choice of market definition is not trivial and will not only
affect the theoretical analysis but will correspond to characteristics and
events in the observable world. In general it is likely that the more
narrowly the boundaries are drawn, the better will be the information
flows but the more insulated the participants in the market will be from
the forces of competition. In the modern world, most firms try to differ-
entiate their products and so to achieve some degree of monopoly power.
A narrowly drawn market is likely to consist, therefore, of a relatively
small number of oligopolistic firms all of which are well informed about
and respond readily to each other's policies. Unless the degree of product
differentiation is small and the number of firms large, it is not very
probable that the prices reached will correspond to the equilibrium price
that would have been set by a competitive market. As the market
boundaries are widened, information passing between firms (and between

buyers as well as sellers) will be less complete and will travel more slowly, but since any one firm's product will have more substitutes, although not such close ones, the competitive pressures will be avoided less easily. The question of market equilibrium is therefore related to market definition, to the time taken for the dissemination of market information and, also to the facility with which resources can be transferred within the markets as defined. At this point in the analysis it would seem that there is hope for the classical case: as long as the markets are broadly defined and the time period is sufficiently extended for adjustments to be completed, tendencies towards a set of equilibrium prices for major markets ought to be established. The period of time required will depend, of course, on the mobility of the factors of production.

It is on this basis that neo-classical macro-economic models, that is modern models of the economy based on the classical tendencies towards equilibrium, have a claim to our attention.

2.6 The Cambridge criticism of the neo-classical position

The neo-classical model of the economy depends for its functioning on the flexibility of prices and on the ability of resources to respond to them. Scepticism about these aspects of the system has been the standard criticism of classical economics for many years, but recently a potentially more devastating critique has been emerged. The line of argument, which has since been developed with both ingenuity and with some ruthlessness towards opponents, began some twenty years ago with assertions[5] that since capital was heterogeneous it made very little sense to talk about the quantity of capital and that there was no real place in macro-economic models for production functions or for choices of process that depended on relating factor prices to marginal products. As the debate progressed, it became apparent that even more fundamental defects were being exposed in the neo-classical position. Even if it were possible to set up a measure of the capital stock in an economy, unless capital was homogeneous and the proportions with which it could be combined with other factors (and in particular with labour) were flexible, the technology used would not be uniquely related to the rate of interest. It appeared to be quite likely that a fall in interest rates might result in a switch to processes that were *less* capital intensive. Even the possibility, and it should be emphasised that it is no more than this, of a perverse relationship between a factor of production and its price is obviously extremely damaging to a concept of economic analysis that depends on prompt and accurate responses to price changes. The debate around the possibility of perverse responses in the choice of technology has become known as the 're-switching' controversy and it is probably fair to say that the Cambridge economists won the contest without great difficulty. The classical market system was shown to be capable of failure at a vital point and also it could no longer be relied upon to give a clear answer to the question of how shares in the total product were determined. Profit has a key role in allocating resources in the classical system, but with factor prices and factor shares left indeterminate, the rate of profit is undetermined. It should be added, also, that if incomes can be misallocated, the demand curves for all products and therefore the vector of equilibrium prices, even given that equilibrium is likely in individual markets, will be 'wrong'.

If the Cambridge case is conceded, little remains of neo-classical macroeconomics yet even while the logic of the Cambridge criticism was being acknowledged, it was possible to talk of 'a neo-classical resurgence'.[6] This was not perversity nor, of course, was it ignorance of the state of play; the fact is that re-switching is only likely to take place under rather special conditions and the occurrence of such conditions was felt by many economists to be rather less probable than those which would lead the system to have more orthodox characteristics. The neo-classical models emerge from the contest definitely more vulnerable, definitely battered but by no means unfit for further service.

Notes and references

1. G. J. Stigler, 'The economics of information', *Journal of Political Economy*, 1961.

2. J. R. Hicks, *Value and Capital*, Ch. V, Oxford University Press, 1939. Hicks took the view that income effects were unlikely to be significant.

3. J. K. Galbraith, *The New Industrial State*, Hamish Hamilton, 1967.

4. See R. Marris, *The Economic Theory of 'Managerial' Capitalism*, Ch. 2, Macmillan, 1964, for a survey of managerial motivation, or J. N. Williamson, 'Profit, growth and sales maximisation', *Economica*, 1965. See also W. J. Baumol, 'On the theory of oligopoly', *Economica*, 1958, for a view that has been very influential.

5. J. Robinson, 'The production function and the theory of capital', *Review of Economic Studies*, vol. 21, 1953–54.

6. The phrase seems to be due to R. Eisner, 'On growth models and the neo-classical resurgence', *Economic Journal*, 1958, but has been much repeated since then.

3
The aggregate economy

3.1 An aggregation of markets

The fine detail of the economic life of a community is much too complex for direct observation to reveal either the general characteristics of the economy or the major tendencies at work within it. An obvious and convenient way of ordering this intricate pattern of human activity is to regard it as a system of exchanges which can be categorised into sets of separate but interacting markets. The behaviour of the economy as a whole is then seen as the behaviour of this aggregation of markets. Market situations arise because of the need for exchange. There is an imbalance between the endowments of individuals, both with regard to their material goods and to the skills and abilities which they possess and this imbalance is rectified by means of exchange. The nature of such exchanges can be discovered by considering first an economy in which only two commodities are traded. This is an extremely traditional device and if the two commodities are named 'grain' and 'wine', fantasies of a pastoral society should not obscure the fact that we are setting up an abstract model of market behaviour. For any one pair of marketeers trading within this simple market economy a ratio will be established at which they are prepared to make an exchange. This ratio will depend on their own personal utility functions and on the quantities of grain and of wine which each of them possesses. If there is no impediment to free trading within the market and if there is full information about the ratios at which trading is taking place, a general market ratio of exchange will be established. There will be a market grain-price for wine and a wine-price for grain. It follows from the nature of exchange that the quantities demanded and supplied are equal at the moment at which trade takes place. That is

$$D_{grain} = S_{grain} \qquad\qquad [3.1]$$

and

$$D_{\text{wine}} = S_{\text{wine}} \qquad\qquad [3.2]$$

It might be noted that since only two commodities are involved, the two equalities are established together. The one set of exchanges provides two demand and supply equations. We also have two prices, either one of which could be treated as the datum-price, or 'numéraire', in terms of which the other is stated.

This approach can now be extended to a more complicated economy composed of many markets. Since they cannot be listed in full detail it will be convenient to suppose that there is some number, N, of commodities and markets and consequently N equations. In this more complex situation, it may be supposed that the quantities demanded and supplied would depend not only on the prices of the particular commodity concerned but also on the prices of other commodities which were complements or substitutes. To some degree the prices of all other commodities will enter into the demand and supply functions, so that a representative equation of the type of [3.1] or [3.2] would appear as:

$$S_N(p_N, p_1, p_2 \ldots, p_{N-1}, W) = D_N(p_N, p_1, p_2, \ldots, p_{N-1}, W) \qquad [3.3]$$

using functional notation. Here p_1 to p_N indicate relative prices referred to some chosen commodity as base and W represents the initial endowments, or wealth, of those trading. The system as a whole could be presented as

$$S_1(p_1, p_2, p_3, \ldots, p_N, W) = D_1(p_1, p_2, p_3, \ldots, p_N, W)$$
$$S_2(p_2, p_1, p_3, \ldots, p_N, W) = D_2(p_2, p_1, p_3, \ldots, p_N, W)$$
$$\vdots \qquad\qquad\qquad \vdots$$
$$S_N(p_N, p_1, \ldots, p_{N-1}, W) = D_N(p_N, p_1, \ldots, p_{N-1}, W) \qquad [3.4]$$

As each of the equations is true by itself, there can be no objection to adding up the right- and left-hand sides to give

$$\Sigma\, S_G = \Sigma\, D_G \qquad\qquad [3.5]$$

where $\Sigma\, S_G$ represents the sum of all the supply equations and $\Sigma\, D_G$ represents the sum of all the demand equations, the subscript, G, indicating that the summed quantities refer to goods and services.

3.2 The possibility of equilibrium in the system

The discussion so far has been interims of quantities rather than of values and the equality [3.5] above, would represent two lists, or vectors, of quantities supplied and demanded. Although the system does not, as described, include money it can easily be recast in value terms, using relative prices based on a numéraire commodity, so that

$$\sum_{i=1}^{N} p_i S_i = \sum_{i=1}^{N} p_i D_i \qquad [3.6]$$

If the demand and supply equations for each of the commodities (equations [3.3] and [3.4] above) are taken to represent buyers' and sellers' marketing plans over a range of prices, then the individual equalities presume equilibrium in the separate markets and the summation of the equilibrium quantities shown in [3.5] is essentially a restatement of the equilibrium of the system as a whole. It is possible, however, for some or all of the markets to clear at non-equilibrium prices and if the symbols S_i and D_i of [3.6] are taken to indicate the quantities actually traded, the equation will be true whether or not equilibrium has been reached. Indeed, when trade takes place it will be necessarily true that the value of goods sold is equal to the value of goods bought and the equality sign of [3.6] could be replaced by the sign meaning 'is identically equal to':

$$\sum_{i=1}^{N} p_i S_i \equiv \sum_{i=1}^{N} p_i D_i \qquad [3.7]$$

It is clear that apart from any more sophisticated criticisms about the appropriateness of looking at the economy in this way, there are at least two areas of doubt, even if this 'general equilibrium' model is taken on its own terms. One such area is whether a system of equations such as that outlined above possesses the *mathematical* properties which are required for a unique solution; another is whether the system considered as an *economic* model, contains mechanisms that would bring about pressures towards equilibrium in all markets. The early discussion centred about the mathematical structure of the system of exchange equations. A very simplistic view of the necessary conditions for a general equilibrium would be that since the system contains N equations, one for each commodity, and since N prices are to be determined, the system must mathematically be capable of producing a unique set of equilibrium prices. This naive approach is upset at once because only $N - 1$ of the equations are independent. Once $N - 1$ demand and supply equalities have been established, the final, Nth, demand and supply equality is determined automatically. In a simple way this has already been demonstrated in equations [3.1] and [3.2] where it can be seen that *one* exchange generates *two* demand and supply equalities. It therefore appears that the system contains $N - 1$ independent equations but that N prices are to be determined, but fortunately the selection of one commodity as numéraire gives a price of unity for the chosen good, so that the required condition of $N - 1$

equations to be solved to determine $N-1$ market prices is finally established.

At this point it is clear that such a system has at least the potential to generate a set of equilibrium prices. The mathematical qualities of the system have not been exhausted by the brief and largely verbal analysis outlined above and a point which has been rather neglected in the literature is that the general equilibrium conditions do not guarantee that the prices produced will be either non-zero or positive. A price of zero would indicate a 'free good', that is a commodity which was not scarce and could be freely enjoyed without entering into exchanges. A negative price would indicate a commodity which some transactors wished to place on the market but which other people would have to be paid to accept. Perhaps, in a situation in which both pollution and resource shortages are important, it would be no bad thing to set out the system of exchanges in a form which could take account of both zero-price and negative-price goods. It is not the purpose of this book to follow up the implications of including such goods within the system of exchanges, however, and so only this mention of their possibility within a full solution will be made.

3.3 Economic equilibrium in the primitive exchange economy

Models of economic behaviour are intended to help us to understand the rather complex processes upon which our material well-being depends and it is obvious that the model outlined in the preceding sections of this chapter is a very primitive and incomplete one. It does show, however, that an equilibrium position in an exchange economy is possible, even though there may be many pitfalls in the way of attaining it. This achievement may be small, but it is not trivial; had even this primitive model not shown the *possibility* of a general equilibrium, the credibility of all exchange or market models, and of the approaches to economic policy which depend upon them, would have been in doubt. There is still a considerable step from establishing the possibility of a general equilibrium to showing that tendencies will be present which will bring about this equilibrium. If it is assumed that all of the many markets are competitive and that information is costless and unrestricted, and if, as well, it can be assumed that all the excess demand curves are downward sloping then tendencies will be at work to correct any movements away from equilibrium that are bound to occur. Any commodities held in excess of a transactor's own requirements will act as 'excess supply', or negative excess demand, and in trading the excess, the transactor will contribute to a lowering of the price of the commodities concerned. Eventually, in a complex modern economy as well as in the primitive one modelled above, 'each person's means of paying for the productions of other people consist of those which he himself possesses'.[1] If any excess supply of commodities *does* automatically provide a demand for other commodities, overproduction of goods or under-utilisation of resources should not be possible. This notion that 'supply creates its own demand' is generally known as Say's law. If J. B. Say's *loi des debouches* carries greater significance than the identity [3.7] (that is that the values of sales and purchases are equal) it adds little to our understanding of competitive markets and certainly does not justify the many thousands of words of commentary that have been devoted to it both before and since Keynes used it as a convenient cock-shy in his powerful attack on the classical economists. Any contribution that Say's law can make to our understanding of general equilibrium emerges only when it is expressed in terms of excess demand. If each individual's demand for commodities arises only because he has commodities to offer in exchange, it follows that at any set of prices the value, in terms of the numéraire, of the goods or services he is offering must be equal to the value of those which he is demanding. The sum of the value of excess demands must therefore be equal to the sum of the value of excess supplies. Considering excess supply as negative excess demand, the sum of the values of all excess demands in the system must be zero.

Writing the excess demand for the 'ith' commodity as x_i, a symbolic version of Say's law, expressed in terms of excess demands would be:

$$\sum_{i=1}^{N} p_i x_i = 0 \qquad\qquad [3.8]$$

In this form Say's law does contribute to an understanding of the nature of general equilibrium and offers a picture of a pattern of excess demands, some positive and some negative, operating across the system of markets to bring about the equilibrium.

3.4 Equilibrium in a money economy

Although the primitive model expresses some true and useful things about an economy based on market exchanges, it is clearly deficient in at least two major respects. The first is the very obvious one that prices are related to money in a real economy and not to some datum commodity. The second is that most *individuals* are exchanging factor services, rather than tangible commodities, for other commodities. While there may be no objection to considering these services merely as commodities for exchange on an equal footing with other commodities, they do have some special characteristics which make it more effective to deal with them separately.

In the primitive model transactors were assumed to have no special reasons for treating the numéraire commodity in any way differently from other commodities; its use as a reference by means of which relative prices could be expressed was merely a convenience and any other commodity would have done as well. As soon as a unit is introduced which has other characteristics of money and can, for instance, be used as a store of value, this simple approach must be abandoned. People have a variety of reasons for holding money and the quantity which they wish to hold may vary as economic or personal conditions change. If the model is extended to allow individuals to vary their money holdings at will, there is no longer any guarantee that the demand for and supply of goods will be equal, even at equilibrium prices, nor will the values of the excess demands for goods necessarily sum to zero when markets are out of equilibrium. What will be true will be that the sum of the values of excess demands of goods and money taken together will add up to zero. This rather less demanding restriction on the system of demand and supply equations is often known as Walras's Law.

The movement of the whole system towards general equilibrium now seems much less sure. People may decide to hold money rather than to buy goods and unless some mechanism to provide compensating effects in the markets for goods can be introduced into the model, the functioning of the market system is again in doubt. Patinkin[2] has suggested that a 'real balance' effect may come into play when such a disequilibrium exists. In the primitive model, there was no concept of a general price level, only relative prices had any meaning. Once money is introduced, however, it is possible to conceive of a level of money prices of goods in general. When there is, for instance, an excess supply of goods and an excess demand for money, so that people want to hold more money but do not wish to take up all the goods on offer at current prices, it is not unreasonable to suppose that prices would tend to fall. Patinkin's real balance effect would indicate that people were alert to the actual purchasing power of their money holdings and that with falling prices they would be prepared to reduce their nominal money balances. The movement towards equilibrium is once again an orderly one, with money balances being reduced as falling prices induce people to purchase more goods until excess demand is zero for both goods and money.

Although this device goes a long way towards restoring the plausibility of the concept of equilibrium in an exchange economy in which money plays a part, it still leaves important questions unresolved. The introduction of money opens the way for lending and borrowing and also adds a further 'price', the rate of interest, since it is not to be supposed that people will lend (even in a model economy) without some recompense. If, without going into too much detail, a market for bonds and a price of bonds is added to our existing markets, Walras's Law becomes

Excess demand for goods

> plus

Excess demand for money

> plus

Excess demand for bonds

is equal to zero, or, in symbols

$$p_g x_g + p_b x_b + x_m = 0 \qquad [3.9]$$

where p indicates price and x represents excess demand. The subscript g indicates 'goods', b indicates 'bonds' and m, money. There are no summation signs because the market for 'goods' is considered as a single 'composite market' and the other two excess demands refer to single markets.

3.5 A more complete model

The general equilibrium model as so far presented illuminates some aspects of economic activity but is not complete enough to provide a basis for the discussion of current problems. The market for 'goods' can be taken as representing all the goods and services which are exchanged and should be disaggregated to show the markets for factor services, particularly for labour, separately. There is also a case for separating the markets for consumer goods and capital goods. The arbitrariness of this last separation is acknowledged but, as we have seen in an earlier discussion, all market boundaries are to some extent conceptual rather than real. At this stage the model will consist of five 'composite markets', each of which represents, at macro-economic level, the effects of many thousands of micro-economic transactions in the commodity group concerned. The five markets produced by these rearrangements will be those for

Consumer goods
Capital goods
Labour
Bonds
Money

In line with our previous reasoning, these markets should produce five supply and demand equations, of which four will be independent. At the level of aggregation, therefore, four prices should be determined by the model. The model in this form should be capable of handling the major questions concerning the behaviour of a closed economy. Like the Keynesian models, which are discussed in the next chapter, it is capable of further extension so that government is allocated a more active role than the creation of money and it can be opened out to permit a discussion of the effects of foreign trade. The question is whether the use of a neo-classical general equilibrium model is likely to lead to different conclusions from those which would follow from the application of the by now conventional Keynesian models.

3.6 The equilibrating process

The general equilibrium model as outlined contains very strong implications that equilibrating tendencies will be present, but it says nothing about the nature of the process by means of which an equilibrium might be reached. The problem of the equilibrating process is more important in macro-economic analysis, where the markets are highly aggregated than in smaller scale analysis where interpersonal bargaining has more credibility. This is a long-standing problem, which Walras approaches through the celebrated theory of *tâtonnement* (that is of groping, or of feeling the way). He saw the process beginning with a random selection of prices (*'prix criés au hazard'*) which are adjusted through an 'auctioneer' as inter-mediary, until all excess demands are eliminated. This seems an extremely artificial device, but it is only an analogy of the way in which market forces operate and, as such, it is an apt one. A modern parallel, which would probably be quite acceptable would be to regard the market as acting like a giant computer, analysing information from intending transactors and arriving through an iterative process, at a vector of prices at which all excess demands were zero.[3] However, there is still no assurance that the *tâtonnement*, or the computer, will arrive at an equilibrium position nor that the equilibrium will be a stable one. All the problems of stability of equilibrium, both within single markets and between markets, remain. A great deal of attention has been paid to the question of the stability of general equilibrium systems[4] and although many of the conditions which can reasonably be expected to hold in a market economy are likely to contribute towards a stable equilibrium others, such as the existence of complementarities in demand, may not do so. Writing at a time of quite rapid inflation, it would be unwise to state with much firmness that the stability of equilibrium could be taken for granted.

Even if equilibrating tendencies are present and the danger of instability in the system is small, it is still possible that the speed of adjustment towards equilibrium will be slow. In the real, as distinct from the modelled world, this would be likely to lead to high levels of unemployment persist-ing over long periods of time as the labour market made only sluggish adjustments towards its equilibrium position. A further result, and a not unlikely one, might be that in a turbulent international trading environ-ment, the national economy would be disturbed, and a new disequilibrium position set up, before the progress towards equilibrium had been completed.

3.7 Models and economic perspectives

A consideration of the characteristics of general equilibrium models supports neither an easy belief in a smoothly self-adjusting market system nor a rejection of the market economy in favour of a centrally directed system. The complications discussed in this chapter suggest that equilibrating tendencies may be frustrated in many ways and that even a system which embodies many features that conservative politicians and businessmen would consider desirable, or would claim for Western economies, may be slow in adjusting after disturbances or may experience occasional periods of instability. Neither post-war experience nor the inter-war depression can be quoted in refutation of general equilibrium models as tools of economic analysis. General equilibrium economics becomes apologetics only when it is presented in its most crude and naive forms. Unfortunately, it is these crude forms which are usually taken as representative and are attacked and ridiculed by critics. In its more sophisticated versions, its failings are that too little attention is paid to the dynamics of the mechanism by which equilibrating forces are applied and that the general equilibrium format is more appropriate to an exchange economy than to one in which the production process is important. Serious and informed criticism of the market system and of mixed systems in which public and private sectors interact may lead to new insights and to new policy prescriptions. Premature rejection of market-based models of economic behaviour is likely to give false perspectives of the economy and to produce policy recommendations which are unhelpful or even dangerous. Perhaps the 'Keynesian revolution' was such a premature rejection, or perhaps the Keynesian models have become so dusty from years of uninspired exposition to undergraduates that their real significance has been lost.

Notes and references

1. J. S. Mill, *Principles of Political Economy*, Book III, Ch. XIV.

2. D. Patinkin, *Money, Interest and Prices*, Ch. III, Harper and Row, 1965.

3. D. Patinkin, op. cit.

4. An enormous amount of technical work has been carried out to determine whether a competitive general equilibrium is likely to exist in the type of system outlined and whether the solution found will represent a stable equilibrium. Contributions by Wald, Arrow and Debreu and Hahn have been important.

4
The new orthodoxy

4.1 The Keynesian pedigree of the standard model

In contrast to the general equilibrium approach, undergraduates have, for many years, been taught macro-economic analysis by means of a standard model which both teachers and students believed to reflect some of the most significant aspects of Keynes's thought. After the publication of Axel Leijonhufvud's *On Keynesian Economics and the Economics of Keynes*, it became fashionable, while still continuing to use the standard model, to claim that it was untrue to the spirit of Keynes's major writings. Although this claim may have been justified in respect of some special features of the model as taught it could not be sustained as a whole, for the essential skeleton of the standard income—expenditure model is quite clearly set out in the *General Theory*. In describing the effects of an increase in the money supply, Keynes outlines a sequence which corresponds closely to the causative patterns traced out in Fig. 1.2 (p. 7).

> The primary effect of a change in the quantity of money on the quantity of effective demand is through its influence on the rate of interest. If this were the only reaction, the quantitative effect could be derived from the three elements — (a) the schedule of liquidity preference . . . , (b) the schedule of marginal efficiencies, which tells us by how much a given fall in the rate of interest will increase investment, and (c) the investment multiplier.[1]

Keynes then considers secondary effects and in particular the effects of resource constraints as full employment is approached, but he goes on to point out that 'the schedule of liquidity preference itself depends on how much of the new money is absorbed into the income and industrial circulations, which in turn depends on how much effective demand increases . . .'.

The links between the real goods and monetary sectors are thus established. The causal chain outlined is, in fact, a recapitulation of a less compact statement of the system which Keynes has made a little earlier in the book[2] and after each of these expositions of his scheme he draws attention to the 'extreme complexity of the actual course of events' and is clearly very aware of the dangers of the mechanical and insensitive manipulation of economic models.

As is well known, the system described can be expressed in the form of two relationships between income and the rate of interest and the ease with which this can be done has no doubt led to the glib and oversimplified analysis which Keynes abhorred. The first of the two relationships locates equilibrium positions in the market for goods and services. In its most simple form, this follows the lines already sketched out in Chapter 1, that is:

(a) with investment given, the flow of income will be established at a rate determined by the saving function $S = f(Y)$ and by the (ex-post) saving-investment equality;

also

(b) the level of investment will depend upon, and will vary inversely with, the rate of interest.

The second of the fundamental relationships in the standard model determines equilibrium positions in the monetary sector. The factors involved here are:

(a) the rate of interest is determined by an interaction between the demand for money (the liquidity preference schedule) and the supply of money;
(b) the demand for money will increase (the liquidity preference schedule will shift to the right) as National Income increases.

In this scheme, the rate of interest is the link between the real goods and the monetary sectors and if both relationships are to be satisfied, there must be a single equilibrium rate of interest and level of income.

Although all the links in this chain of reasoning are present in the *General Theory* much else is there as well, since Keynes was as much concerned with human behaviour in economic affairs as with exactly specified mathematical relationships. The result is that Keynes considered a much greater variety of economic effects than are present in the specification set out above, but that he did not always follow through the logical connexions between them.[3] The desire to reduce a complex and subtle discussion to a compact logical scheme led directly to one feature of the standard model which has caused much controversy and has been responsible for some obscurity in the subsequent debate. J. R. Hicks, in his famous article designed to discover and contrast the points of difference between classical and Keynesian theory,[4] needed to reconcile Keynes's insistence that the rate of interest was independent of the demand for investment. To do this he suggested, and there were grounds in the *General Theory* for doing so, that some minimum rate of interest existed, which would not be further reduced by increases in the money supply. This would create a region in which increases in the propensity to invest in new capital equipment would increase income but would not affect the rate of interest. It was on this basis that the notorious 'liquidity trap' entered the standard analysis.

4.2 The model formalised

Sir John Hicks's intention was to set out the classical and Keynesian theories in their most stark forms. One of the ways in which he was able to do this was by representing the real goods and monetary relationships outlined in the previous section of this chapter in diagrammatic form. The downward sloping investment (MEC) curve with respect to interest rates, combined with the positively sloped curve relating saving and income and the ex-post saving—investment identity, ensured that the points of equilibrium between income and the rate of interest would lie on a negatively sloped line. In the monetary sector, the rightward shift of the negatively sloped liquidity preference function as income increased ensured that the relationship between income and the rate of interest, with the money supply taken as fixed, would be a positive one, the shape of the curve being determined by the shape of the liquidity preference function. Hicks called the first of these curves the *IS* curve and the second the *LL* curve. The only possible equilibrium in both sectors is given by the point of intersection of the two curves. The usual presentation is as shown in Fig. 4.1, where the notation used is that of A. Hansen, whose commentary on and critique of Keynes's work[5] added much to the popularity of 'IS—LM analysis' and gave some further prestige to the idea of the liquidity trap. In the Hicks—Hansen presentation, monetary influences are ineffective only at low income levels and interest rates, that is in the Keynesian 'special case' conditions. This is the situation illustrated in Fig. 4.1*a*. If the assumption that investment is interest-inelastic is added, the situation is exacerbated so that even at higher interest rates and income levels changes in the money supply will leave investment and income very little affected. These more severe assumptions are shown in Fig. 4.1*b*.

4.3 Policy analysis and the attractions of *IS—LM*

The wide acceptance of the standard income—expenditure model as the

Fig. 4.1   The *IS—LM* model

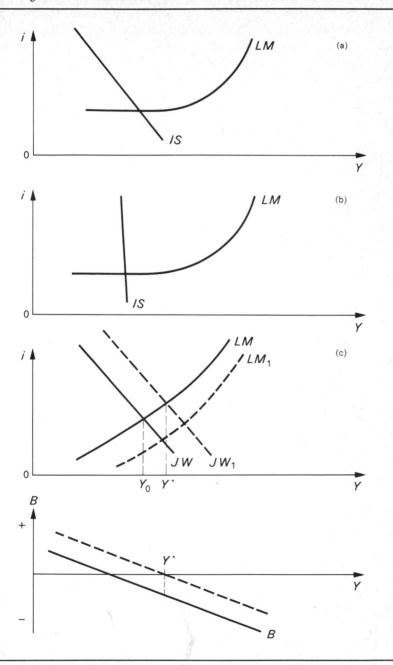

basis for analysis at many levels, at that of the student, of the academic economist and of the policy analyst, has been partly due to the compactness of the way in which a complex set of ideas has been presented and partly to the adaptability of the format within which they are expressed. An example of this second feature is the ease with which the simple version given above can be adapted for quite realistic policy discussion. An alternative way of introducing the fundamental Keynesian concepts is to do so in terms of the 'circular flow of income'. In this terminology, investment is an 'injection' into the flow of income and saving a 'withdrawal'. Injections, naturally, tend to increase the flow of income and withdrawals to reduce it. Equilibrium is reached when there is no tendency for the flow of income either to increase or to contract, that is when injections are equal to withdrawals. The *IS* curve can thus be considered as the line showing all the possible positions at which injections and withdrawals are equal. If we are contemplating the addition of other injections and withdrawals, this curve, giving not investment-saving, but injection-withdrawal equalities could be called the *JW* curve. The additional injections which must be included are Government Expenditure on goods and services and Exports; the additional withdrawals are Taxation and Imports. The '*JW*' equilibrium positions are arrived at when

Investment
plus
Government
Expenditure   are equal to   Saving
plus   plus
Exports   Taxation
                                 plus
                                 Imports

It is perhaps worth saying that the equilibrium condition no longer requires that investment equal saving, nor for that matter that government expenditure equal taxation nor that exports equal imports. Unbalanced budgets and non-zero balances of payments on current account are permissible; all that is required for equilibrium is that injections in the aggregate are equalled by the total of withdrawals. A *JW—LM* model is shown in Fig. 4.1c, complemented by an external balance function, showing the balance of payments position to be expected at various levels of economic activity. In this particular diagram, the solid line in the balance function shows an adverse balance at full employment, the level of activity indicated by Y^*.

The usefulness of this model, and the dangers of its simplifications, will be readily apparent and are no doubt so well known that it would be tedious to rehearse them at length. Increases in any of the injections will move the *JW* curve to the right, reductions in injections or increases in withdrawals will shift it to the left. Increases in the money supply will move the *LM* curve to the right and reductions to the left. Under-employment equilibrium positions are possible, as shown by the solid curves, and attempted equilibria to the right of the full-employment position, as indicated by the dotted curves, will lead to excess demand and to inflation. Rising prices will tend to reduce the effective money supply and will move the *LM* curve back to the left. In the balance of payments diagram, devaluation, or its equivalent in terms of a floating currency, will lead to a raising of the balance function, again shown by a broken line. Corresponding positions of the *JW* line will depend on the new policy mix which accompanies the increased flow of exports relative to imports (and on the relative prices of those components of the aggregate).

A surprising number of the policy packages that have been applied during the last twenty years can be analysed in terms of this diagram; it is small wonder, in view of the ease with which its elements can be acquired, its apparently respectable pedigree and its practical usefulness, that it has become part of the working economist's basic tool-kit. The danger lies in the elements which are implicit but unstated and in the many very impor-tant things which are omitted from the analysis.

4.4 A critique of the new orthodoxy

The important and distinctive feature of Keynesian models is that they permit the existence of equilibria at levels of activity which are not suffi-cient to provide full employment. This feature is present in modern Keynesian formulations, such as that described above, only when very special assumptions are made. The Classical view of the economy is that if there is equilibrium in all markets, including that for labour, no one who is willing to work at the equilibrium real wage need be out of a job. If there is unemployment, it must be either voluntary or 'frictional' and the latter should, if the economic system is working efficiently, be of fairly short duration. Some unemployment, of course, might be more difficult to cure if major changes were taking place in the industrial or regional pattern of economic activity, but even this 'structural' unemployment would be a problem of adjustment and the appropriate policies for its treatment would be those which eased and assisted the necessary structural change. In contrast to this view, the standard Keynesian models suggest that 'involun-tary unemployment' can exist even when money and goods markets are in equilibrium. However, the standard model described earlier in this chapter says nothing explicitly about the labour market, but as a theory of employ-ment it carries the implication that the demand for labour depends on the level of aggregate expenditure. This leaves entirely open the question of why low levels of employment and output are not corrected by adjust-ments in the real wage. It is not usually suggested that market forces are absent so far as labour is concerned, although it is widely accepted that trade union activity may make them less effective than they might otherwise be. If this is the only barrier to an adjustment towards equilibrium, then the standard $IS-LM$ model is almost empty of analytic content, since even the purest classical model would produce unemployment if market forces were not permitted to function. Provided that the tendencies towards equilibrium lead to higher output, falling prices, with the real balance effect, should revive total demand. If the standard model is now to provide a convincing explanation of the existence of situations of unemployment equilibrium, the interest-inelastic IS-curve and the liquidity trap become essential. The crucial nature of the liquidity trap in the Keynesian argument was realised by Hicks — 'the most important thing in Mr Keynes book' — and has been remarked upon by many subsequent writers, but even if there were satisfactory empirical evidence of its existence, the liquidity trap is a low income-level phenomenon and a more general validity is claimed for Keynesian theory than that of mere 'depression economics'. The evidence for the unresponsiveness of the IS-curve, too, is mixed and many modern studies[6] indicate that investment, and probably other elements of total demand, are to some extent interest-elastic. On this interpretation of the Keynesian and Classical approaches, the distinction between the two views seems to be spurious and, it may be supposed, the emphasis on the manipulation of aggregate demand that follows from the acceptance of Keynesian policies equally misguided. In spite of the apparent success of demand management in the post-war years, it is quite possible to point to heavy defence and aero-space expenditures as more important determinants of prosperity and to argue that policy interventions by government have been counterproductive.[7]

It is clear that the flexibility of prices and the responsiveness of intentions and outcomes to them is at the heart of the matter, but the standard Keynesian model encapsulates a discussion which is conducted in 'real' terms. In this, as in many other aspects of the analysis, modern interpreters follow Keynes, although he converted from a money basis by re-valuing the aggregates in wage-units, whereas the more usual practice today is to suppose that money values are deflated by appropriate price indices. Whilst this device is necessary for some comparisons and can be handled with a proper discretion in a verbal analysis, it can be dangerous when the argument is conducted largely in terms of a simple diagrammatic analysis. The only price-effect which is displayed on the standard $IS-LM$ diagram is the movement of the LM curve as price changes lead to variations in the real, or 'effective', money supply. This almost total silence of the $IS-LM$ model with respect to prices has a further outcome; the model can have little to add to the analysis of inflation, its only contribution being that prices will tend to increase as aggregate demand exceeds the full employment income level. Even more damaging to the claims of the model to be in any sense a complete and logical scheme is its complete inability to deal with situations in which income is relatively low but prices are rising rapidly, that is situations of 'stagflation'. The model is also inadequate for a sensitive analysis of response to price and interest rate charges in another respect. Since the model is a short-period one, the degree of response depends on the unit time period chosen. This problem is not an unfamiliar one in ordinary market analysis, but in macro-economic models the situation is complicated by the fact that the response times are likely to be different in the various sectors of the economy. This means that the choice of time period may be critical in determining the predictions which flow from the model. The difficulty is compounded by the fact that the unit time period used is often undeclared.

At this point, it must be admitted that the 'standard model', the $IS-LM$ diagram with or without appendages, does not seem to be in good shape and yet it is extremely effective for the analysis of policy in a practical way and many economists who are not committed to a neo-classical position are reluctant to abandon it. As Professor A. G. Hines has put it, 'The classics won the intellectual battle; Keynes won the policy war'.[8] The last few years have made both victories seem less secure.

4.5 An appraisal of rival orthodoxies

The intellectual victory of the neo-classical school, which seems to have been very widely accepted during the 1960s and early 1970s, is valid only if the contest is fought on the classical economists' own ground and only if it is conceded that the classical system itself is appropriately expressed within a neo-Walrasian framework. The neo-Walrasian criticisms have inflicted great damage on the foundations of the standard Keynesian model, and this is not to be regretted to the extent that it has called into question certainties that were based on inadequate analysis. One reason why the standard model, battered though it may be, is not abandoned by economists may be that the neo-classical victory is conceded only on the narrow neo-Walrasian grounds and that this is felt to be a limited success which has left the main fields of economic analysis untouched. Economics is a discipline which is closely concerned with the lives and prosperity of ordinary people and with the dynamics of the societies in which they live. An admission of total victory to the neo-classical school would involve, if intellectual integrity is to be at all meaningful, an admission that the appropriate economic policies to be followed were those which gave the most freedom to market forces. Such policies would limit intervention to the curbing of monopoly power, to the regulation of the monetary system and to the provision of support in a few areas of activity in which the market could not be expected to operate with efficiency or with the necessary minimum of compassion required in a civilised state. This would involve exchanging the new Keynesian orthodoxy for an even older and far less acceptable one. An alternative way out of the dilemma, advocated with great panache by a small group of economists who consider themselves to be Keynes's true heirs, is to find a new way forward by going back to Ricardo (aiming a vicious and damaging blow at the neo-classicals on the way by attacking the uniqueness of the relationship between factor prices and the optimum factor mix in the production process). If the neo-classical ascendancy is seen to depend on the acceptance of a strict correspondence between the elements of the Keynesian models and those of the general equilibrium aggregate market models, neither a complete dismantling of the Keynesian scheme nor a resort to extreme solutions may be necessary. The neo-Walrasian correspondence between the two models of the economy depends on an implicit assumption that the time periods contemplated are equivalent in both models, that the functions which appear to represent the same relationship in fact do so and that 'equilibrium' means the same thing in both cases. Once the standard Keynesian model has been equipped with an aggregate production function and a labour market in which the demand curve is given by the marginal productivities of labour derived from that function, the meaning of equilibrium at full employment can be agreed by both parties to the dispute. The nature of the demand functions in the two models is not quite the same. In the Keynesian models, expectations and an awareness of the importance of future states have more significance than in the classical model, which, having its roots in the exchange economy is more concerned with *intentions*, or static plans to buy or sell which will be implemented at market clearing prices. There is also room for discussion about the market structure of the Keynesian model. It is quite clear that this structure must consist of more than the money and goods markets which are shown in the Hicks–Hansen diagram. The addition of the labour market is necessary for the debate to begin and since the liquidity preference function implies, at least in so far as the 'speculative' demand for money is concerned, a demand for bonds there must also be a concealed and undeclared bond market. This hidden bond market will be in equilibrium when the money market is in equilibrium and the equilibrium price of bonds will be inversely related to the rate of interest. With these assumptions made, the equivalence of the market structures is complete; the standard Keynesian model is, in effect, a four-market general equilibrium model.

This rough equivalence of the two systems occurs only if *all* the necessary assumptions are made, however. It is rather like the focusing devices fitted to some cameras; when the lenses are exactly adjusted, the two images overlap and form a single projection in the viewfinder. The Keynesian and neo-Walrasian systems overlap only when all the adjustments have been made and one remains to be considered, the unit time period. Since it has been an underlying concern in this book to keep alive the idea that the principal, and perhaps only, reason that macro-economic models are important is that they offer guidance in the formation of economic policy and the assessment of its results, it is suggested that an appropriate time period would be one which is related to policy objectives. For most practical purposes, this would indicate a time period too short for a neo-classical, or neo-Walrasian, adjustment to be completed. As was pointed out in an earlier chapter, these are large, aggregate markets with many imperfections in their sub-markets and the movement towards equilibrium is unlikely to be rapid.

Neither model emerges from this comparison entirely unscathed and neither offers an explanation of *how* movements towards equilibrium take place. The coincidence of the two systems, on reasonable but not the only possible, assumptions makes it even more urgent to investigate the market process in an economy in which there is no *tâtonnement* and no Walrasian auctioneer.

Notes and references

1. J. M. Keynes, *The General Theory*, Ch. 21, p. 298.

2. J. M. Keynes, op. cit., Ch. 18.

3. This is not to subscribe to the view that Keynes's work was inconsistent, but see A. Hansen's famous commentary *A Guide to Keynes* (McGraw-Hill, 1953) especially Chs 7 and 8; and also Leijonhufvud's comments in the Introduction to his *On Keynesian Economics and the Economics of Keynes*, especially p. 15 et seq.

4. J. R. Hicks, 'Mr Keynes and the Classics: A suggested interpretation, *Econometrica*, 1937.

5. A. Hansen, op. cit.

6. R. G. Hines and G. Catephores, 'Investment in UK Manufacturing Industry, 1956–67' (in *The Econometric Model of the United Kingdom*, eds K. Hilton and D. F. Heathfield, Macmillan, 1970) find interest rates to be a significant variable in the explanation of investment, but with a considerable time lag. M. S. Feldstein and J. S. Flemming, 'Tax policy, corporate saving and investment behaviour in Britain', *Review of Economic Studies*, 1971, also find that the effect of interest rates is statistically significant. Neo-classical models of the type pioneered by

D. W. Jorgenson indicate that it is so but employ a composite variable, the implications of which are not easily disentangled for our purposes.

7. A very critical view of earlier policy is given by N. Macrae in *Sunshades in October*, Allen and Unwin, 1963.

8. A. G. Hines, *On the Reappraisal of Keynesian Economics*, Martin Robertson, 1971, p. 9.

5
A revised view of Keynesian economics

5.1 The missing excess demand

During the preceding chapter it emerged, in spite of quite determined efforts to avoid such a conclusion, that the Keynesian model had no obvious features which would distinguish it from neo-classical, general equilibrium models. Provided only that the unit time period was sufficiently long to permit the equilibrating forces to do their work, and provided that no impediments to equilibrium such as rigid prices or wages were introduced, the excess demands or excess supplies should exert pressures in the expected way. The market structure of the standard Keynesian model is ordinarily concealed by the style of its presentation, but it exists nevertheless. If there are differences between the two systems, they are to be found not in the aggregate market structures, although that of the standard Keynesian model is excessively simple, but in the assumptions which are made about the processes by means of which equilibrium is reached. The same conclusion follows even if the Keynesian model is taken to be appropriate only for the short period, for then it becomes necessary to show that the unemployment, or, indeed any other disequilibrium phenomenon which occurs, is exempt from correcting pressures. Only if it is so exempt do policies which are intended to maintain aggregate demand artificially become necessary.

One indication that all may not be as simple as this is given by a consideration of the case of unemployment disequilibrium about which much of the debate has centred. Suppose that the level of aggregate demand, determined by the interaction of the goods and money markets in the Keynesian manner is too low to provide full employment. In the standard Keynesian analysis this is a position of unemployment *equilibrium* and from the Walrasian point of view, too, the goods, money and bonds

Fig. 5.1   The labour market and the 'missing' excess demand

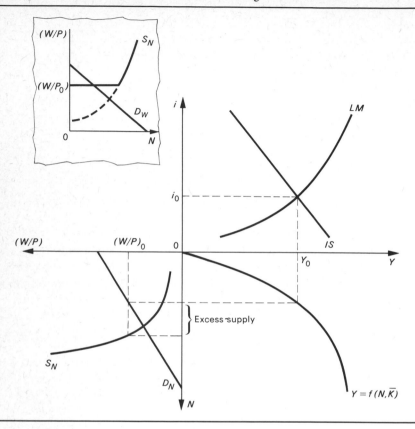

markets are in equilibrium. If the low level of economic activity is fundamentally due to excessively high wages, however, real wages will be above the equilibrium level for the labour market. The position will be that shown in Fig. 5.1, with the labour market out of equilibrium, there being an excess supply of labour. From the Walrasian point of view, somewhere in the system there should be a corresponding and counter-balancing excess demand, but it is not to be found. In the absence of this excess demand, the adjustment of the system to a full employment equilibrium seems uncertain and even the nature of the system is no longer clear.

5.2 Some suggested solutions
One explanation of the absence of an excess demand for goods, money or bonds even though there is an excess supply of labour would be to deny that the unemployment was truly involuntary. If the trade unions are

strong enough to prevent any workers from offering their labour services below a certain wage, the labour supply curve may assume the form shown in the inset to Fig. 5.1. The perfectly elastic, horizontal, section of the supply curve, intersects the demand curve at a comparatively low level of employment. The implication here is that those workers who are unemployed, even if they are not members of trade unions and are not loyal to union ideals, are either unwilling or afraid to violate the unions' minimum wage policy. This simply does not ring true for the depression years and as a theoretical argument is merely another version of the 'rigid wages' explanation of the occurrence of unemployment. If the trade union wage constraint is relaxed, it is possible to envisage processes which would lead to full employment with lower wages encouraging increased production. This would bring about, eventually, a lower level of prices and, perhaps with the help of real balance effects, a corresponding increase in the demand for goods. Real balance effects, as Archibald and Lipsey made clear some years ago,[1] cannot be relied upon to increase consumption permanently although they may assist in the progress towards equilibrium. Whatever process is invoked, however, it must be one which absorbs the excess supply of labour, translates it into excess supplies in other markets and eventually dissipates it as the economic system approaches full employment. In the real and observable world, it requires great optimism to believe that entrepreneurs will expand output in the way required to initiate the process merely on the realisation that they can employ cheaper labour. In the model, however, they are taken to be profit maximisers with perfect information and so may do so.

Such a process as that described is only approximately Walrasian and many of the disturbing effects discussed in Chapter 2 may come into play. Whatever sequence of adjustment is proposed, and this will depend on the speed with which prices change in the various markets, it seems unavoidable that there should be a period in which unemployment persists and wages are quite far from their equilibrium level. During this time, the income effects may be important, since the operation of the Walrasian homeostat depends on the volume of trading at non-equilibrium prices being small. If this is not the case, some people's incomes will be increased, as compared with what they would have been at equilibrium, and others' will be decreased. This is very much the position under conditions of prolonged unemployment and in the years of depression before the Second World War, those in employment found life good, with prices tending to be low as compared with wages and houses, for example, very cheap. Hardship tended to be localised, both geographically, in that certain areas and industries suffered more than others, and also with respect to particular sections of the community and even individuals. As Hicks pointed out in

Value and Capital, the behaviour of markets in which income effects are too large to be ignored becomes very uncertain and the ordinary analytical apparatus breaks down. Since the situation with which we are concerned seems to be one in which income affects must be taken into account, and in which their influence cannot be mitigated by the intervention of a Walrasian auctioneer who will conveniently prevent false trading 'at non-equilibrium prices', some alternative analysis must be found.

If we are neither to gloss over the problem of the missing excess demand, nor to make over-convenient assumptions about the adjustment process, we could follow a line of thought suggested by Clower.[2] This approach would be to acknowledge that there would be an excess demand for goods and services, to correspond in value terms with the excess supply of labour, if the unemployed workers enjoyed the incomes which they would have had at equilibrium. Since they do *not* have these incomes there exists only a *notional* excess demand.

5.3 The dual-decision hypothesis

The dual-decision hypothesis is the name given by Clower to the pattern of decision making producing the result outlined above. It is an hypothesis only, not a description of actual behaviour since it is concerned with one possible way in which consumption decisions could be made. Keynes repeatedly stressed the importance of the consumption decision in his scheme and Clower takes up this point, going so far as to say that Keynes must have had a dual-decision hypothesis at the back of his mind 'or most of the *General Theory* is nonsense'. Keynes certainly emphasised that decisions to consume were constrained by actual income and to that extent Clower may be right although there is perhaps little profit in attempting to imagine 'what Keynes really meant' when direct evidence does not exist. It is important to explore ideas that deepen our understanding of macro-economic processes, though, and the dual-decision hypothesis may help to put Keynesian and Walrasian approaches into relation with each other and to give some clues about the behaviour of both systems in disequilibrium situations.

The idea which underlies the dual-decision hypothesis is the conventional one that households attempt to maximise utility subject to a budget constraint, this constraint being set by their expected incomes. Under conditions of full employment equilibrium, there is no problem; expected incomes are achieved. If the economic system fails to reach full employment equilibrium, then some households will find that their expected, or notional, incomes are less than their actual incomes and so they must maximise utility by rearranging and reducing their expenditure to conform to the constraint imposed by their actual incomes. This seems fairly straightforward and unexceptional, but it must be remembered that the ordinary demand curve carries the implication that income remains constant. The only sensible interpretation of this condition is that quantities demanded will not be affected by income changes in the neighbourhood of equilibrium. There is a good deal of evidence, such as that contained in the work of Duesenberry, of Friedman or of Ando and Modigliani, to show that consumption does not vary directly with current income and it seems likely that fairly small changes in income will not affect spending on consumption goods and services. When there is considerable unemployment, however, we leave the neighbourhood of equilibrium and reductions in current income become significant for many people. When, under these conditions, household consumption decisions are aggregated to give the demand for consumption goods and services for the community as a whole, the implications of the dual-decision process can no longer be disregarded. If the dual-decision hypothesis is accepted, the problem of the missing excess demand is cleared up at once; the supply of factor services is still 'notional', that is the labour supply curve is unchanged and there is excess supply at the going real wage but there is no excess demand for goods and services since it has been eliminated by the reallocation of expenditure to meet the constraint of reduced, realised incomes. Clower states quite firmly that it must follow that Walras's law is operative only at equilibrium, but this would mean that it did not function as an adjusting device at all. If the values of excess demands and excess supplies are equal only at equilibrium, they are equal only when they are all zero. This is to deny that this version, at least, of the classical market mechanism operates at all. Perhaps this is too sweeping; it accords better with observation to allow market mechanisms some validity and to suppose, as suggested above, that they become ineffective and distorted when deviations from equilibrium become at all gross.

5.4 The dynamic adjustment process

The view set out above, that the dual-decision hypothesis is appropriate when large deviations from equilibrium occur, is consistent with the concept of the market as an information system. This idea and the concept of search behaviour which follows when information is imperfect were briefly discussed in Chapter 2. Within this information context, it is reasonable to suppose that when deviations from equilibrium are small buyers and sellers in all markets see conditions as normal. If this is so, and if they are not mistaken in their belief that nothing unusual is happening in the market, their information is likely to be good and their expectations accurate. Perhaps, in modelling such a situation, it would not be inappropriate to use a permanent income approach to consumption in the fashion

of Friedman and in that case there would certainly be no significant reduction in expenditure so long as small changes in current income were seen as
transitory. In a well-explored and relatively stable situation price changes
are perceived and, if deviant, are corrected by changes in the flows of
purchases. When there are real changes in market conditions, due perhaps
to the introduction of a lower-cost process, the rearrangement of purchases
tends to bring about a new equilibrium price. Price, in short, is able to do
its job as a signal of either aberrant or changed conditions and as a stimulus
to ensure that an appropriate correction or response follows. As soon as
conditions become very different from normal, this happy and convenient
situation ceases to exist and the stability of expectations even contributes
to the subsequent collapse, since it leads to a failure to adjust to a changed
demand for labour services. Once the pattern of prices becomes dispersed,
it is difficult for transactors to know what is going on. Recent developments of Stigler's approach to market search, such as those reported by
L. G. Telser[3] indicate that search becomes much more rapid and effective
when the shape of the distribution of prices is known. It seems likely that
the further the current market situation diverges from equilibrium, the less
will be known about the distribution of prices and the longer will search
behaviour continue, with consequent delay in adjustment.

It is this kind of situation which Leijonhufvud has in mind when he
discusses the process by which income-constrained decisions, on the Clower
pattern, might operate in an unemployment disequilibrium. Sellers of
labour services are seen as having a 'reservation price' on their own services,
that is a value below which they would rather retain their time and skills
under their own control than sell them on the market. Leijonhufvud says:

> Consider a seller of labour services who finds his old employment
> terminated. The seller will not change his reservation price instantly
> but will first attempt to ascertain that the decline in sales was not
> simply a random event. . . . The unemployed worker . . . may start
> with a reservation price close or equal to his old wage, turning down
> employment opportunities which promise lower wage rates. As his
> search progresses, his sample of employment offers gets larger and the
> maximum wage offered increases.

If the termination of employment is due to a general decrease in demand
or if the worker's occupation is one which is no longer required to the
same extent as before, the maximum wage offered is unlikely to be as great
as his former earnings even though his search is very long. Also, as
Leijonhufvud points out, information about jobs available is expensive to
acquire not only directly but also in terms of earnings foregone. As in other
models involving search behaviour, the process will go on until the gain

from an expected better offer is estimated to be less than the costs involved in further search. None of this is inconsistent with the position taken earlier that in the years of high unemployment, workers would, on the whole, not have insisted on wage levels unrealistically far above equilibrium. When unemployment appears, workers' expectations are based on previous information and experience and are revised only as new information becomes available. In times of severe economic recession it seems likely that this 'inelasticity of expectations' would be relaxed more quickly as it became clear that work was hard to find.

The process outlined above might seem to have some self-correcting aspects, since the deeper the depression, the more quickly will expectations be revised. This would be to ignore not only the absence, or possible absence, of any balancing excess demand for goods and services but also the secondary effects of reduced incomes during the period of search. It is here that the multiplier, which has a rather weak role in modern macro-economic theory, is restored to its former importance. The income-constrained consumption decisions of workers who are searching for jobs commensurate with their reservation prices for their own services will be on a much more modest scale than their expenditures when they are in employment and this will lead to further reductions in demand. The result of this secondary fall in demand will be income-constrained decisions for another set of people and so on, the multiplier becoming, in Leijonhufvud's phrase, a 'deviation amplifying process'. There is a further consequence to this collapse of demand. Even when the process settles down, as the successive rounds of downward adjustment become smaller, the set of prices ruling at the unemployment equilibrium will be a very different one from that which would have existed at a classical full employment equilibrium. From the point of view of market equilibrium, this will be an incorrect set of prices and so the information which the 'price vector' transmits to potential buyers and sellers will also be incorrect. Under these circumstances, the forces which would restore the system to its equilibrium position seem to be wholly lacking.

One more aspect of the adjustment process ought to be considered. At various places in the foregoing discussion of the process of adjustment towards market equilibrium it has been suggested that the reaction times in the various markets are important. In all the neo-classical schemes, assumptions are made which smooth away this problem. In the Walrasian *tâtonnement*, prices are called and offers and bids are adjusted until quantities supplied and demanded equate. In Marshallian markets the assumption, largely implicit, is that changes in demand or supply conditions are instantly reacted to by a change in the equilibrium price. It is not enough to acknowledge, as Hicks does, that 'false trading' may exist and that it may give rise to difficult situations, the situations envisaged by Clower and developed by Leijonhufvud are ones in which the existence of inelastic expectations and the relatively slow acquisition of correcting information make trading at non-equilibrium prices the dominant feature of the market. Information failures are likely to reverse the classical order of reaction times, so that prices change rather slowly with the consequence that it is the quantities traded that must adjust.

5.5 Keynesian models and the new view

The approach to macro-economic analysis discussed above is thoroughly modern in that it concentrates on decisions, on expectations, on the transmission and reception of information and on the nature of processes occurring within the structure of a complex system. Models based on such an approach are likely to be superior to those which depend on more restricted versions of economic behaviour. If Clower and Leijonhufvud are correct in their interpretation, Keynes great contribution was in showing how this type of analysis could be applied to an economy which was out of equilibrium in the Walrasian sense. On this interpretation, Leijonhufvud's hostility towards the standard income—expenditure model is more than justified, since it ignores the most valuable part of Keynes's economic scheme, the processes which underlie the rather obvious surface relationships. Because *IS—LM* models rely on comparisons of static positions with a minimum of discussion of the decisions made by transactors, of the varying reaction times involved or of the changing information content of different economic situations, the standard Keynesian model represents a step backward from the *General Theory*. Once the processes of adjustment of the system are ignored, or are assumed to be orthodox market pressures of the Walrasian or Marshallian type which are frustrated in some way or other, Keynesian models become vulnerable to attack by general equilibrium theorists.

A further shortcoming of the standard Keynesian model which has been pointed out by those who wish to rehabilitate the true economics of Keynes as against that of his successors, is that the aggregative structure of the standard model is not the same as that which is implicit in Keynes's own work. As we have seen, the standard model uses a four-market, three-price structure, investment goods and consumption goods being together subsumed into a single 'output' variable. Keynes, to the extent that he thought and wrote in terms of market structures, certainly did not use this one. In the *General Theory* he is extremely critical of attempts to measure the 'National Dividend' or to use the concept of a general price level. However, Keynes was a man of his time and both the quality and quantity of information and also the means of handling it have improved out of recognition in the intervening forty years. Also, Keynes objections were largely practical, not theoretical, and he says that he believes that a concept of net real output is 'the right and appropriate concept for economic analysis'. Criticisms of the aggregative structure are on stronger ground if they relate to the adjustment process in disequilibrium situations and the absence in many presentations of the income—expenditure model of a market or a price for capital goods may misrepresent the nature of the investment decision or the division of total output between capital and consumption goods. Leijonhufvud's suggestion is that the correct interpretation of Keynes's implied aggregative structure is to put together not capital goods and consumption goods, but capital goods and bonds as a single non-money asset. This is convenient in that it provides a single rate of interest which is the reciprocal of the price of the 'non-money asset', but it is not helpful in establishing a model for policy analysis and it obscures the enormously important distinction between physical assets, with all their implications for raising the capacity constraint on total output and for the transmission of technological change, and non-physical ones. The argument that Keynes found it convenient to follow a certain line of analysis is not a reason for continuing to do so in perpetuity.

Two other aspects of the Keynesian analysis which are illuminated by the new approach deserve mention. The independence of saving and planned investment comes about because decisions to save provide no information about future consumption plans. There is no 'intertemporal price vector' that would enable businessmen to discover what revenues might be expected from outlays on new equipment. Similarly while command of money balances confers the power to acquire goods and services and so to influence price, decisions to increase money holdings are a planned denial of information about future expenditure intentions.

5.6 A basis for future work

The new view of the Keynesian analysis is very convincing and fits well with recent work on consumer behaviour and business decision making at the micro-economic level. To accept this much need not involve the rejection of the standard Keynesian models however; the real criticisms of the income—expenditure type of analysis concern the way in which it has been misused, the crude assumptions which have been embodied in it to ensure that an unemployment equilibrium was attained and the concealment of the processes and structures on which the too familiar relationships depended. It could be argued that the new view itself is little more than a sophisticated, and on the whole successful, attempt to explain wage and price rigidity and to make them respectable, but this would be a wilfully narrow verdict. The concentration on states of unemployment disequilibrium has probably been inevitable given the general tenor of the Keynesian debate over the years, but a full application of the new analysis requires that it be extended to other situations. It is not enough to point to information failures; in some markets and at some times information will be good and reaction times fast.

If the income—expenditure model is to be retained, extended and used in a more understanding way, it will be necessary to pay more attention than has been customary to the underlying decisions and structures. It will be necessary above all to be very aware that each comparative static 'snapshot' corresponds to an instant in the dynamic sequence and that the dynamic process itself must be well understood. Some of the development towards this understanding may come from the application of empirical findings, as for example in Hines's and Catephores's work on interest rates and the lag structures in investment functions,[4] but new theoretical work and the evolution of new tools of analysis will also be required.

Notes and references

1. G. C. Archibald and R. G. Lipsey, 'Monetary and value theory: A critique of Lange and Patinkin', *Review of Economic Studies*, 1958.

2. R. W. Clower, 'The Keynesian counter-revolution: A theoretical appraisal' in *The Theory of Interest Rates*, eds Hahn and Brechling, Macmillan, 1965.

3. L. G. Telser, 'Searching for the lowest price', *American Economic Review*, 1973.

4. A. G. Hines and G. Catephores, 'Investment in UK manufacturing industry', 1956—67' (in *The Econometric Model of the United Kingdom*, eds K. Hilton and D. F. Heathfield, Macmillan, 1970).

6
Models for disequilibrium analysis

6.1 Some requirements for the analysis

The Keynesian and classical analyses are both, in their usual forms, concerned primarily with situations in which there is equilibrium in the market for goods and services. This concentration on states in which planned expenditure is necessarily equal to the value of goods and services produced makes it extremely difficult to deal with circumstances in which this apparently natural, and even inevitable, condition does not hold. The usual analytic devices, including most mathematical models, are designed to discover and display these equilibrium states and consequently carry too little information about non-equilibrium situations to give an improved understanding of current problems or to help in discriminating between alternative policies. The fact that judgments have been made before the models were constructed does not matter if testable hypotheses can be derived from them, but usually this is not the case.

A disequilibrium in the market for goods and services must mean that the total of planned expenditures is not equal to the value of the total output which is being offered for sale at the prevailing price level. When total expenditure falls short of the value of goods and services being offered, goods remain unsold in warehouses and on the shelves in the shops. This furnishes a very clear signal to businessmen that their present policies ought to be modified and if the quantities of goods unsold are large, will encourage a rapid revision of their expectations. Changes in business policy are likely to include both price reductions, in order to clear stocks and to maintain liquidity, and downward revisions of future production plans with probable reductions in workers' incomes. It is not possible to say that either of the alternatives of price or output reduction will be followed exclusively, nor is it easy to predict which of them will predominate in the economy as a whole. Where, as in much of manufacturing industry, oligo-polistic market structures are the rule, there may well be a reluctance to cut prices and this will tend to make a Keynesian rather than a classical adjustment likely.

In situations in which planned expenditures at the current price level exceed the value of goods and services offered for sale, the signals to businessmen and manufacturers will be in the lengthening lists of unfilled orders and in the quickening flow of business. Under these conditions, there has been little sign of a reluctance to increase prices nor of trade unions to use the situation as an opportunity to bid up wages. Whether upward revision of production plans also follows will depend on how long the good times continue. Most recent work on industry's investment decisions suggests that a fairly sustained period of good trade is needed before industry is persuaded to increase capacity.[1] More intensive use of existing plant, even in the short run, is very probable, however. Since a variety of response to situations of temporary excess demand or excess supply in the goods market is possible, our macro-economic model ought not only to be able to break away from the convention of using compara-tive statics only to hop from one equilibrium situation to another but also to analyse alternative adjustment processes. There are definite advantages in considering alternatives within a common format, since the use of models with quite different structures to handle alternative assumptions introduces the possibility of confusing differences between the systems being compared with those which are implicit in the analytic method. The very thorough demonstrations, some of which were discussed in Chapter 4, that Keynesian and general equilibrium models have a common structure when in equilibrium seem to offer a starting point for development. The emphasis of the common model would have to be changed, however, so that adjustment processes rather than equilibrium states become the main focus. The analysis would also have to take account of varying information flows and the reactions to them, since the modern approach to macro-economics suggests that this is where the real difference between the systems lies. It also goes without saying that any model which is used must take account of monetary effects, both in order to reflect changes in monetary policy and also to allow for the secondary effects of adjustments in the goods market.

6.2 A simple disequilibrium model

It is generally accepted that decisions to consume and decisions to invest are both capable of being taken independently and that while they are subject to economic influences and constraints they are also affected by non-economic pressures which have their basis in the psychology of the decision makers. In the case of investment, these non-economic, social and personal influences become important because of the uncertainty and the lack of information which surrounds the decision and in particular because of the lack of an inter-temporal price vector that would link current saving decisions with future expenditure decisions. It is less generally accepted that similar, though not so powerful, considerations affect the production decision. Individual decisions about output levels are taken without precise knowledge of demand functions and even firms with full information about their costs and a determination to maximise profit may find that they make gross miscalculations of sales. Although it may sometimes be convenient to assume that these production errors cancel out in the aggregate, this cannot be taken for granted. Production decisions have to be taken in advance of sales, for the most part, and as with investment there is not a flow of information linking the future sales period with the present period in which the decision is made. The probability of aggregate production being at some level other than the optimum, classical equilibrium one is increased once expectations as well as non-equilibrium prices are admitted as disturbing influences. Such disturbances are likely to be not merely random ones which might not matter greatly in the aggregate, but will be likely to bias all production decisions in the same direction, since all producers will be receiving similar market signals. In the absence of very full information flows and near-equilibrium prices, independent production decisions may conform to neither classical nor Keynesian patterns. The classical model requires production decisions to conform to profit-maximising outputs with the equilibrium real wage equalling the marginal product while the Keynesian one sees production and employment as being dominated by aggregate demand rather than being determined autonomously, since demand adjustments through price changes are virtually ruled out.

As a first step towards introducing some, but not all, of these ideas into a macro-economic model we could assume the independence of the production decision and see what consequences might follow. This would not necessarily mean that the decision was totally unrestricted and it could hardly be free of the restraints imposed by the state of technology in the society concerned. Nor could it mean that the decision process was entirely unstructured; some entrepreneurial or managerial objectives must underlie the decisions which, in total, produce the observed macro-economic output levels. In the absence of strong evidence that other objectives are appropriate, that of profit maximisation will be retained. This can be interpreted to mean that with a given real wage, the collective result of production decisions is to give a total output at which the marginal product of labour just equals that real wage. This will be so whether or not the real wage is an equilibrium one determined by market forces. In situations in which businessmen see the level of output as being restricted by demand, the usual flow of causation may be reversed, so that the output decision determines the labour requirement. The production decisions described above determine the volume of total output offered for sale and so give aggregate supply.

Since the model is intended to handle simple disequilibrium situations, aggregate demand must be determined quite separately from output. In line with the requirements for a disequilibrium model set out earlier in the chapter, it is suggested that the influences on aggregate demand should be the familiar Keynesian ones, with the total value of goods and services demanded being the result of expenditure decisions. The analysis is conducted in 'real' terms in the sense that all outputs and expenditures are valued at constant prices. In disequilibrium, total factor incomes will be determined by expenditures and not by the value of output, which may remain unsold. The component of income which is likely to be reduced in that case is profit. The multiplier may be taken to work very much in the usual way so far as its effects are concerned, but should be thought of as operating through the processes discussed by Leijonhufvud so that reductions in employment lead to reduced consumption expenditure and so to further income-constrained decisions. The autonomous elements in the system are government expenditure on goods and services, taxation and the money supply. The question of whether government, working through monetary institutions can control the money supply with sufficient effectiveness and flexibility to have a successful monetary policy is left for later discussion; for the purposes of the model it is assumed that control is possible. Investment is determined in the usual way and is therefore semi-autonomous in the sense that entrepreneurial expectations and confidence affect the marginal efficiency of investment. It may be appropriate at this point to draw attention to another element of independence between the expenditure and output decisions. Decisions to order investment goods will result, in the case of major outlays, in payments being made to factor owners well in advance of the new equipment becoming available or of payment being made for it. Whether this is important depends to some extent on the length of time period chosen for analysis and, in practical terms, on whether progress payments are made in the course of the work. Whenever *changes* in the rate of investment are made, however, the possibility arises of discrepancies between aggregate supply and aggregate demand being caused by factors of this kind.

The model described is of a closed economy, so that for the moment there is no need to deal with the complications caused by foreign trade. The working of this closed economy is divided into two major sub-systems, but these are not isolated from each other. Changes in the price level, responding to the existence of excess demand or excess supply between the two sub-systems, and the level of employment incomes are the two most direct links by means of which the sub-systems interact with each other, with expectations providing connexions of a more tenuous kind.

6.3 Formal presentations of the model

The component parts of the economic system are shown in Fig. 6.1, where it can be seen that each of the two main sub-systems is composed of two subordinate sub-systems. The aggregate supply sub-system consists of an employment sub-system and a production sub-system (those who prefer to call these lesser parts 'sub-sub-systems' may do so); the aggregate demand sub-system has an expenditure sub-system and a monetary sub-system as its subordinate parts. To trace out all the links between the systems would be a tedious repetition of the verbal explanation of the previous section, but the conventions used may need some explanation. The arrows show the direction of the effect which one sub-system has upon another and the symbols indicate which element produced by the sub-system is responsible for the effect. Thus the employment sub-system produces a real wage (W_R) and a quantity of employment (N). The volume of employment acts as an input to the production sub-system which has aggregate supply as its output. The other relationships are all as previously described and are all in real terms. 'Prices', including the real wage, and the interest rate, are shown in octagonal boxes and quantities are shown in the square boxes. Three points may need further explanation although they have been indicated in the previous discussion. The first is that N and W_R together give a value ($N \cdot W_R$) to the real value of incomes from employment (the dot notation indicates multiplication) and this is shown as affecting aggregate demand, an effect which is subsequently discussed in detail. The second point concerns the influence of aggregate demand on production during periods of contraction. At such times, the influence of decisions taken within the employment sector may be over-ridden by the direct effects of expenditure limitations. In the diagram this is shown by the connexion from the Expenditure box to the Production box through the circled-V symbol. This symbol indicates that *either* the effect from Employment *or* that from Expenditure can influence the volume of production but not both. A possible point at which an expenditure-dominated process could switch-in would be when firms' production is limited by liquidity problems and current, and falling, revenues were their only source of funds. The final point concerns expectations (E), which reflect not only influences from outside the economic system but are also affected by the size of the total wage bill, since, considered as a cost this will reduce the residual profit,

Fig. 6.1   The economy in outline

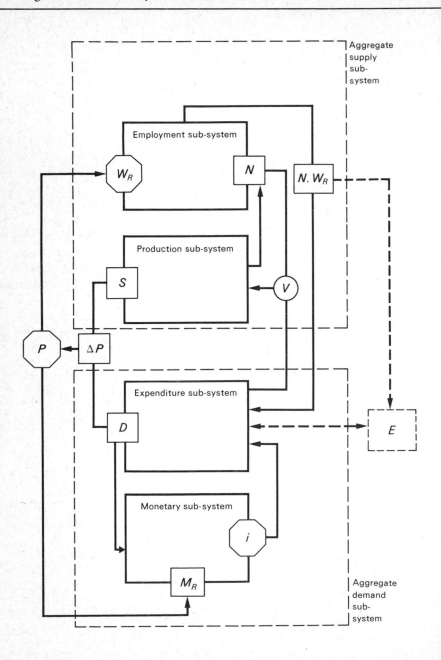

and by total expenditure which represents revenues to firms. The remaining symbols are largely self-explanatory but are in any case included in the list given below.

The processes involved when an economic system is out of equilibrium may be seen more clearly when the fine-structure of the various sub-systems is considered. This is shown in Fig. 6.2, but before any further discussion the symbols used in the diagram are listed, so that the rather complicated diagram may be followed more easily.

Symbols used in block diagrams

C	total consumption expenditures
C_1	the element of consumption which is determined by aggregate demand
C_2	the element of consumption which depends on the size of the wage bill
D	aggregate demand
E	business expectations
G	government expenditure on goods and services
G_{NET}	government expenditure, as above, less taxation
I	investment
i	the rate of interest
Δi	the change in the rate of interest
M_D	the quantity of money demanded
M_{D1}	the part of the demand for money which depends on total expenditure (the 'transactions demand')
M_{D2}	the part of the demand for money which responds to the rate of interest (the 'speculative demand')
M_S	the money supply (actual, not price corrected)
$M_{S(R)}$	the effective money supply ($= M_S/P$)
N	the volume of employment
N_D	the quantity of labour demanded
N_S	the quantity of labour supplied
P	the price level
ΔP	the change in the price level
S	aggregate supply
T	taxation; T_1: taxation responding to the level of income T_2: taxation independent of the level of income
W	the wage rate (in money, not real, terms)
W_R	the real wage ($= W/P$)
ΔW_R	the change in the real wage

Excess demands:

D_X	(aggregate) excess demand in the market for goods and services

Fig. 6.2   Inter-relationships in a closed economy

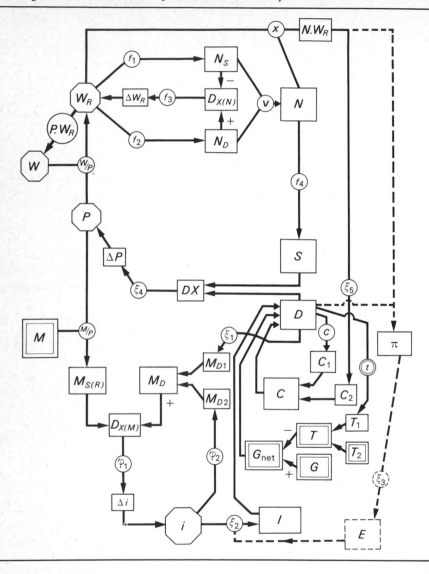

$D_{X(H)}$ excess demand for money
$D_{X(N)}$ excess demand for labour

Functional notation:
This indicates dependency, which may not be linear and may indicate a
complicated relationship between the variables concerned.

f_1 to f_4 functional relationships in the aggregate supply major sub-system.
ϕ_1 to ϕ_3 functional relationships in the monetary sub-system
ξ_1 to ξ_5 functional relationships between elements in different sub-systems
c the marginal propensity to consume; a linear relationship
t the proportion of income taken in tax.

Note:
With the exception of M_s and W, all values are to be taken as deflated to real, or constant price, terms. Similarly, the rate of interest is a real rate adjusted to allow for the rate of change of prices.

    The upper part of the diagram shows the aggregate supply sub-system and the lower part, the aggregate demand sub-system. The two components of the aggregate supply sub-system are a labour market and a production function and the conventions used are a straightforward extension of those which were applied in earlier block (or control) diagrams. Direct arrow connexions indicate additive relationships (subtraction where negative signs are shown). Thus quantities supplied and demanded generate excess demand:

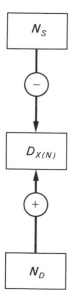

Links which include one of the functional signs show that the two elements are connected in a more complicated way and the direction of the arrow shows which way the dependency runs. Thus the quantity of labour supplied depends on the real wage offered and so the arrow points *from*

60

the wage *to* the quantity supplied. The *supply function* is therefore
represented as

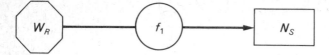

and the points which satisfy this relationship would form the labour supply
curve if plotted. The functional relationships f_1 and f_2 determine supply of
and demand for labour and these give rise to excess demand (which, of
course, may be positive or negative) which, through f_3, brings about a
change in the real wage (ΔW_R). This, the diagram indicates, is to be added
to, or subtracted from when there is excess supply, the real wage. The
revised real wage feeds back through f_1 and f_2 until the excess demand is
reduced to zero and a stable value of the real wage is attained. The process
is just a little more complex than it appears, since the real wage depends
on the combined effects of the money wage and the price level. With
constant prices, the pressure falls on the money wage and excess demand,
for instance, will result in a bidding up of the money wage and so of the
real wage. Other kinds of disequilibrium events are possible, however. An
equilibrium in the labour market may be upset by a rise in prices which
will reduce the real wage and if reactions to this are not very fortunately
timed some very unhappy adjustments may follow.

The labour market is linked to the production function in two ways.
The market process itself generates the quantity of labour which is to be
combined with existing stocks of other factors in the production process.
This is shown by the quantities supplied and demanded being linked
through the circled V symbol. In equilibrium, N_S and N_D are equal and so
either will serve to generate N. Out of equilibrium, it is assumed that the
quantity demanded will dominate. The other connexion between the
employment and production sub-systems is through the two functional
relationships f_2 and f_4. The demand function for labour is the marginal
productivity function (or more strictly its inverse, so that labour is the
dependent variable) derived from f_4, the production function. These
connexions ensure that the labour market decisions follow the lines set
out earlier. Having described one market process in some detail, the
remaining price and quantity determining systems can be followed very
easily. There are two other circuits laid out in much the same way, that
for determining the rate of interest and the one which initiates changes in
the general price level when the main aggregate demand and aggregate
supply sub-systems are out of line. Changes in the price level feed back
through the effective money supply and the real wage to induce correcting

changes in the major sub-systems. Reading Fig. 6.1 and Fig. 6.2 together, the relationships and inter-connexions should be clear. To put the system into motion requires judgments to be made about the delays which might occur in the various responses. If we merely make the easy assumption that all prices and quantities are fully flexible and responsive, with no significant leads or lags, then the system represented will behave like a very well-ordered general equilibrium one and will always give full employment and the profit-maximising level of output that goes with it.

6.4 A scenario for the collapse of a classical equilibrium

To gain some familiarity with the model, a relatively uncomplicated situation is now analysed. Since the model deals with processes and can represent alternative adjustment paths, it is necessary to specify very carefully, within the conventions of the model, what is happening. Following earlier discussion, it is assumed that small deviations from equilibrium leave expectations and expenditure plans largely unchanged. A not very large fall in employment, with a consequent small reduction in the total of incomes derived from it, would not then lead, through the link from N . W_R to C_2, to significant reductions in consumption and in aggregate demand. The functional relationship ξ_5 can easily be specified in a way that allows for this and we may assume that this has been done. An alternative way of specifying the model so that small deviations did not set disequilibrating processes in motion would be to set up response thresholds, as has been suggested in other models of economic behaviour.[2] This would be appropriate and could be justified in the case of employment income and consumption expenditure, moreover it would have the required stabilising effect, but similar thresholds elsewhere in the system might be very destabilising.

As a first examination of processes at work when the economy is jolted out of equilibrium it might be well to extend the case discussed above. Suppose that either trade union action or some temporary disturbance or information failure in the labour market leaves the money wage unduly high by comparison with the price level, so that the real wage is well above equilibrium. It is absolutely necessary to specify clearly what delays occur in subsequent reactions and to say unambiguously in what order events occur. Here, we shall suppose that as the increase in the real wage is considerable, that first of all the business decision makers perceive it, that they consider it significant and that they decide to reduce output and employment. The process begins at W and W_R, therefore, and proceeds first along the labour demand route, via function f_2 to N and so to S. Although there will be an excess supply of labour $(-D_{X(N)})$, it will not operate to correct the real wage while the newly unemployed are searching for jobs at their old, and high wage rates. In the sequence discussed in Chapter 5, the period of search led to a fall in consumption, so this time it will be assumed that the second event, which will follow before any other corrective action can take place, is that reduced incomes do act, through function ξ_5, on consumption C_2 which reduces aggregate demand, D, and so sets the multiplier circuit in action. If the reduction in aggregate demand equals the initial fall in aggregate supply before any further reactions are induced, the situation discussed in the previous chapter and illustrated in Fig. 5.1 will have been reached. Although this situation, with excess supply in the labour market uncompensated by excess demand in the goods market, is a possible outcome and one that is much discussed in the literature it does not look so stable and permanent when discussed in this context as it does in the comparative static models. It is reasonable to assume that the time period during which each new situation is played out is quite short, perhaps three months would be a suitable period to have in mind. This will mean that investment expenditures during the period are too small to have any discernible effect on the factor mix or the production function. If this is so, a disequilibrium sequence initiated by an increase in the real wage will have not only the primary and secondary effects which we have discussed but a tertiary effect due to the fall in total net revenues (in the circumstances outlined this is a necessary consequence). These lower net revenues, following the path through ξ_3 in the model, will affect business expectations and consequently investment decisions. Making the very arbitrary supposition that the primary effects of each major event take one-quarter of a year to work themselves out, it is possible to set a rough time scale on the sequence. Three months after the initial increase in the real wage, which threatened profits and forced a cutback in output, and employment, business again finds sales volume falling everywhere as are profits. At the end of six months this has become serious enough to undermine business confidence and so expansion plans are cut back during the third quarter after the initial disturbance. This seems a not unlikely beginning to a serious recession both as regards the time scale and the sequence of events. It is probably at this stage that the situation will tend to become politically and socially unacceptable and that government intervention will become inevitable. Market forces alone are not likely to bring about a revival; even if the unemployed workers have already revised their reservation prices and are willing to accept lower wages, all the signals coming in to business are bad and neither the prospects of future profit nor the working capital to finance an increase in production are likely to be present. It is in situations such as this that the homeostatic devices in the system may cease to operate or may transmit signals that are interpreted perversely by decision makers. Consideration of a scenario for this more disastrous type of collapse is deferred until Chapter 7.

6.5 A simplified method of analysis

Although the block diagrams enforce a consideration of the processes at work within the economic system they are a little complicated, particularly in the fine-structure form. Also being concerned only with processes, they say nothing about the state of the economy and of its various sub-systems at any one time. This is unavoidable in a model which is not designed to show only one sequence of events and so does not converge on a well defined single outcome. There would be advantages if a more compact way could be found of presenting the influences at work and the sequences of events which must be traced out. In terms of the equations linking the variables in the system, although not of the way in which they are used, the system as presented follows very familiar lines[3] and it is suggested, therefore, that a variant of the $IS-LM$ diagram could be adopted as a convenient device for keeping track of progress through a chain of events and their consequences. Used in this way, with a labour market and production function included in the presentation, the diagram would be a kind of ideogram which called to mind the concepts involved without representing them fully. It would be necessary to split the horizontal axis into two parts, so that aggregate demand and aggregate supply could be shown separately, with the possibility of indicating a disequilibrium in the goods market. The diagram proposed is illustrated in Fig. 6.3 and this form of analysis is used, at first in conjunction with the block diagrams, in Chapter 7. The partitioning of the system in the diagram alters the nature of the IS curve so that it represents not true equilibrium points in the system but only income—expenditure equilibrium at the current price level. Since the money market is a rapidly adjusting one, the intersection of IS and LM curves *may* indicate the level of aggregate demand although time may have to be allowed for expenditure decisions to respond to changes in interest rates. Assuming for the moment that time lags can be ignored, the intersection of the two curves will give the expenditure intentions of business, government and households at a particular interest rate and a given price level. These plans are shown in constant price terms and if supply, on the lower axis in Fig. 6.3, reacts exactly and immediately to changes in aggregate demand the analysis becomes the familiar $IS-LM$ one. If for any reason supply cannot adjust, other processes must be invoked. The nature of the reconciliation between aggregate supply and aggregate demand is no longer specified by the model itself, however. If prices are flexible and respond freely to excess demand or excess supply, the model will reach a classical equilibrium. One way or another, in the

Fig. 6.3   The generalised (*IE–LM*) model

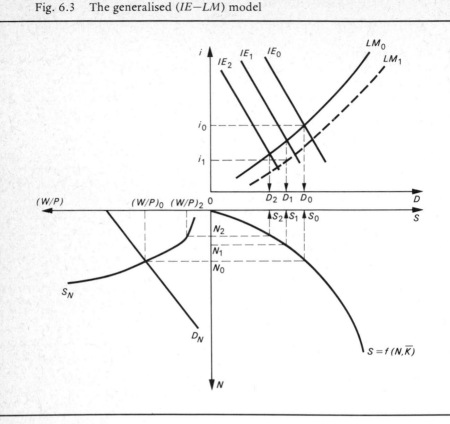

course of the analysis, the two aggregates must be brought into agreement and while price or quantity adjustments are all that the diagrammatic analysis allows for, transferring the discussion to a more practical field may require consideration of the existence of stocks and of changes in them.

The need for conscious discussion of the form of the reconciliation process focuses attention on the dynamic nature of the equilibrium concept. While equilibrium itself seems a static concept, it necessarily entails the idea of departure from equilibrium positions and of balanced forces which maintain the equilibrium. The relationship which always exists between a comparative static analysis and the concealed dynamic process which determines the equilibrium and may sometimes upset it, is often referred to as the 'correspondence principle'.[4] The separation of expenditure and output decisions enforces a choice as to which underlying dynamic process is the appropriate one and permits consideration of factors not shown explicitly in the diagram.

In order to emphasise the changed character of the analysis and to prevent an automatic assumption of supply adjustment, the income—expenditure decision curve has been given the symbols IE rather than IS in later discussion.

Notes and references

1. R. Eisner, 'A permanent income theory for investment: Some empirical explorations', *American Economic Review*, 1967, and for the United Kingdom N. H. Dimsdale and A. J. Glyn, 'Investment in British Industry: A cross-sectional approach', *Bulletin of the Oxford University Institute of Economics and Statistics*, 1971.

2. N. E. Devletoglou has suggested that such thresholds may be of significance in some aspects of consumer behaviour, see *Threshold and Rationality*, Kyklos, 1968.

3. An example of such a model is given in simultaneous equation form in Appendix I.

4. P. A. Samuelson, *Foundations of Economic Analysis*, Ch. IX, Harvard University Press, 1947.

7
Economic models and the real world

7.1 Economic depression and the plausibility of models

If an economic theory cannot survive the harsh touch of reality, it must be discarded. Keynes's rejection of the classical vision of a well-ordered and self-adjusting economic system was justified because it could easily be seen that the economy was not behaving in the way required by the theory. Once events have shown that a model is not an appropriate representation of the economic system in even one particular situation, it loses its claim to general validity and this was certainly the case with the classical scheme in the 1930s. In Britain, the economic situation was much more like the one considered in the previous chapter, with money wages and the price level out of step but with income-constrained expenditure decisions frustrating movement towards a full-employment equilibrium. Certainly the figures show that prices fell much more rapidly than wages and salaries during the period 1929 to 1932, so that the real wages of those remaining in employment increased. During these same years, output fell by about 6 per cent, but it recovered after 1932 so that by 1939 Gross Domestic Product (at factor cost and constant prices) was some 20 per cent higher than it had been ten years earlier. The figures conceal millions of personal disasters, of course, and in the early 1930s the number of unemployed doubled but this, too began to improve as the decade progressed. The whole period, and the decade which preceded it, was a time of disgraceful mismanagement but the economy was not totally out of control and even if the war had not imposed its own solutions, intelligent demand management could have completed the process of restoring full prosperity. The economy was not in a truly pathological state; the lines of communication were still open, the system still functioned and was on the way to recovery in spite of insensitive and inappropriate policies.

The income-constrained process analysed in Chapter 6 suggests a sequence of events which can lead to an under-employment equilibrium in which the classical tendencies are frustrated, but in the real world such equilibria are mere pauses in a sequence which cannot stop. In the United States the depression was deeper, attitudes and expectations were more severely upset and the recovery was much less certain so that unemployment was still at depression levels right up to the rearmament boom that followed the outbreak of war in Europe. The loss of confidence after the stock market collapse led to cuts in investment expenditures year after year until by 1933 gross private investment in fixed assets was little more than a quarter of the 1929 figure. Using the split-axis income—expenditure and production model (Fig. 6.3) we can envisage a disequilibrium being set in motion by a reduction in demand sufficient to ensure that the classical homeostatic devices do not operate. This means that the IE curve moves to the left so that all income expenditure points require lower interest rates. Assuming a rapid adjustment in the money market, a new aggregate demand position will be established where IE_1 intersects with the LM curve. This merely gives the new expenditure position following a sequence of adjustments in the expenditure and monetary sub-systems. The result in this first short period will be a fall in sales as shown by the upper arrow (at D_1) in the diagram. Initially, the production rate for the period having been set by decisions in the previous period, there may be no reductions in output, but an excess supply will exist between the maintained output level (S_0) and the reduced level of aggregate demand. A 'Keynesian' sequence would see producers reluctant to adjust prices, so that the differences between S_0 and D_1 represents involuntary stockbuilding, an occurrence which sends out very strong signals that output should be reduced. The process of adjustment then becomes demand dominated, so that the lower aggregate supply arrow follows the demand indicator down to S_1 or to a little below in order to eliminate unsold stocks. An alternative opening to the sequence of adjustments would be a 'frustrated classical' one in which prices are reduced to avoid unsold goods, but the level of output remains unchanged. The consequent rise in real wages will result in falling profits and a reduction in employment and output since the disturbance was specified as being large enough to upset the classical adjustment mechanism. The chain of events is very like that discussed in the previous chapter, but has the difference that since the system has already been nudged out of equilibrium and the increased real wage is part of a reaction to this, the reduction in employment, and employment incomes, will trigger further reductions in consumption and a reduction in entrepreneurial confidence. In Fig. 6.3, the IE curve may be visualised as drifting to the left, from IE_1 to IE_2 and so on, with the output arrow following the demand arrow very closely downward as the system again becomes demand dominated. In all probability a real adjustment process would combine both 'Keynesian' and 'frustrated classical' reactions to the initial fall in demand, but once business confidence is damaged, the processes converge. The process can now be followed on both the first of the block diagrams (Fig. 6.1) and on the split axis income—expenditure—output diagram. In both models the direction of causation runs from the output decision to the labour requirement. In the block diagram, the path runs from the expenditure sub-system through the circled V to the production system, cutting out the influence of the labour market. The causation now runs back to N, as shown by the arrow, and the volume of employment determines the wage to be paid. In the fine-structure diagram (Fig. 6.2), this would require the labour market arrows to be reversed, with the profit maximising decisions of entrepreneurs taking the path of causation from N through the circled V along the upper, supply, function to the real wage, which would thus become the lowest real wage that would secure the labour force required. This is all much simpler in the split-axis diagram, where we can read down from the supply arrow (from S_2, for example) to the production function and so to N_2, the quantity of labour required and then to $(W/P)_2$, the required real wage. Every time we do this, we reduce N . W_R, however, and so reduce consumption expenditures still more setting the multiplier to work again in a new and, by this stage in the process, tragic collapse of demand. Not every detail of the sequence has been fully explored, but the important point is that both the assumption of a rigid-price, Keynesian initial response and a flexible price response lead to the same collapse once business confidence is lost, output is reduced, and the system becomes demand-dominated. Amongst the points that ought to be stressed is that once equilibrium-level decisions are left behind, all the signals coming in to businessmen, of falling prices, falling sales, reduced profits, are pessimistic and encourage further contractions. A further point is that the normally beneficial profit maximising decision becomes malign once falling demand determines output. A legitimate query is whether falling prices in the initial stages (later on as demand and supply are reduced together price falls will be less abrupt) will not act through the effective money supply and lower interest rates to stimulate investment and so to sustain and revive aggregate demand. This seems unlikely when business expectations are far from buoyant and also most of the available evidence suggests a lag of well over a year before lower interest rates have any affect on investment decisions. In Fig. 6.3, the initial price fall might be seen as producing a 'ghost' LM_1 to the right of the original LM curve, thus lowering interest rates to i_1 but not becoming operative on aggregate demand until the collapse was well advanced. It is possible that a delayed response to lower capital costs might, with the need to renew equipment in order to maintain even low levels of output, play a part in revival.

Perhaps this scenario for the collapse of a potentially self-adjusting system is too dramatic even for the United States depression experience in the 1930s, but it has some points which correspond better with the recorded experience than either conventional Keynesian analysis or assumptions of rigid prices and wages in classical models. The sequence described leads to a true economic depression and terminates only with government intervention on a large scale or with real wages reaching a subsistence level below which workers begin to withdraw from the production process.

7.2 Empirical evidence and the construction of the model
In applying the model to an analysis of economic collapse various reason-able assumptions were made about the order in which events took place and about the reactions of decision makers to price and profit signals. Once the distinction between models which have tendencies towards the full employment of resources and those which do not is seen to depend upon such assumptions, it becomes very important to question them and to refer to the evidence where it exists. In the major fields of consumption and investment there has been a great deal of econometric work in recent years and in some respects a consensus is beginning to emerge.

The evidence regarding consumption has been mentioned briefly in an earlier chapter and it is true to say that the view which is now accepted is that consumption does not depend on current income alone but is also influenced by living standards experienced in the recent past. One of the most influential formulations of this view has been Professor Friedman's permanent income hypothesis, which requires consumption to be a weighted average of past income levels, with recent experience carrying greater weight than that of more remote periods. Manipulation of the original formula shows an approximate equivalence with a simple depend-ence of consumption expenditures on current income and the previous period's consumption. While this does not reflect the relationships indicated by the block diagrams, it does not contradict them either, since the several variables related in the disequilibrium model are likely to be correlated when translated into observations. A further difficulty is that observations reflect *outcomes*, when sales and purchases are necessarily equal at the prices which have ruled during the accounting period for the economy, with the valuation of the physical increase in stocks making up any difference in output. Under these conditions, total incomes, including profits, and total expenditures will be equal in the familiar national income accounting sense and the link between employment incomes and an element (C_2) of consumption would not be very readily discoverable using statistical methods. It is not appropriate to discuss or to attempt to review the econometric methods or the current state of investigations in any detail, but two points seem worth mentioning. One is that the muted response of consumption to current income may support the assumption that small deviations from equilibrium may leave the classical adjustment process intact. The other is that there might be advantages, in terms of correspondence with observations, in inserting a lag between $N \cdot W_R$ and C_2 in the fine-structure representation. A reservation which ought to be made is that most of the econometric work ordinarily quoted, that of Friedman, Duesenberry, Modigliani and Ando and so on, is based on American data and that great caution ought to be exercised in transferring results from one economic context to another. In this case such evidence as there is from United Kingdom sources does not conflict with the view given.

In the case of investment there is a great deal of evidence from both British and United States investigations but the trouble is that it is not based on a single theory of the causation of investment expenditures. It may be agreed, on the whole, that early investigations purporting to show the interest-inelasticity of investment have been discredited either because the circumstances in which the evidence was gathered are not relevant to present day conditions or because of imperfections in the statistical methods used. Two main lines of investigation have been running in recent years: a neo-classical approach which would have investment a function of an optimum capital stock which varies with both income and interest rates, and an accelerationist school which sees investment as responding to changes in output as well as to various other, subsidiary factors. In addition many investigators have concerned themselves with the effect of excess capacity on investment decisions.[1] For the British economy, a fair summary of the evidence might be that interest rates do have some effect, but only after a long delay, possibly of about two years (nine quarters is one estimate). Lags are involved in acceleration effects, too, and in general it may be said that only a sustained growth in sales over a fairly long period will stimulate investment outlays. A lag of six or seven quarters between an increase in sales and the consequent increase in investment outlays is a not unusual estimate. In our model, this may be thought of as working firstly through expectations and then through delivery delays, although there are some pitfalls here and from an expenditure point of view the lag may be overstated due to the payments patterns in the capital goods industries mentioned earlier. When there is excess capacity, as at the end of a moderate recession, the accelerator effects will be blunted and it is unlikely that investment expenditures will play much part in the recovery from such a position. On the whole, the evidence relating to investment is in line with the assumptions made in the demonstration of the model at the beginning of the chapter.

Evidence on price movements has been very much concerned with the post-war experience of rising prices and so, both in the data considered and the econometric models used, provides less information about other types of economic experience. As might be expected, excess demand is only one of several factors involved and inter-relationships between wage and price increases have an important part to play in accounting for variations in the rates of increase in the price level. More recent studies indicate that social variables, such as labour militancy, may be significant as, of course, are government policies intended to over-ride labour market processes. Many of these factors are better considered in an examination of inflation, but there is nothing in the evidence to suggest that the type of disequilibrium analysis so far used would be invalidated in this context.

All that is intended in this brief review of current evidence is to run a rapid check-list in order to gain some idea of the way in which a very generalised model of economic processes ought to be operated. Controversial evidence must be incorporated in more specific models and predictions subjected to exacting tests where these can be devised.

7.3 The model and inflation

In many circumstances the model which we have set up will behave in much the same way as a standard Keynesian model. In times of moderate recession, as we have seen, the system will give an unemployment equilibrium which will not deteriorate into a collapse unless businessmen lose confidence, or have no access even to short-term finance, and follow down every small reduction in demand. The model does not give results substantially different from the Keynesian ones if inflation is considered as a phenomenon associated with full employment. The usual way of dealing with inflation in the standard Keynesian analysis is to assume that the full employment level of output marks an absolute limit to the volume of goods and services that can be produced. Attempts to generate expenditures in excess of this level, often shown by $IS-LM$ intersections to the right of the full employment income level on the *conventional* diagram, lead to price increases and to a leftward movement of the LM curve as the effective money supply declines and a new equilibrium is reached. Gestures towards realism would acknowledge bottlenecks as full employment equilibrium was approached during the 'run-up' towards inflation. Used in this way, the IS-curve must have the same meaning as our IE-curve and the process can be interpreted in the same way as long as all measurements are in price-corrected terms. Attempts to express aggregate demand in excess of full employment level in money terms require a different format and other complications are introduced since we may find that an implicit 'money illusion' has been introduced into expenditure decisions.[2] This view of the inflationary process as being associated primarily with attempts to run the economy too close to capacity output has undoubtedly been appropriate at some times, particularly in the early post-war years, but by the end of the 1950s there were sufficient instances, in a number of countries, of inflation being associated with output below capacity or with an absence of excess demand, for its validity to be called into question. Nevertheless, anti-inflationary policies continued to be framed in terms requiring not only a reduction in aggregate demand but also reductions in output. It may have been the case that many policy makers had become so conditioned to think in conventional Keynesian terms that the two concepts seemed synonymous. The standard Keynesian approach to inflation over simplifies in another way which could be important. The assumption that there is a cut-off point for output at the full-employment level either rules out the labour market altogether or it is based on a production function in which the marginal productivity of labour becomes zero after the full employment point is reached. Alternatively, the assumption may be that there is a market for labour but that the supply of labour is perfectly inelastic in the neighbourhood of labour market equilibrium. One possibility is that none of these assumptions is correct but that a highly oligopolistic industrial sector, with tendencies towards sales revenue maximisation, is operating at outputs well beyond the profit maximising point that would define full employment in the classical sense. This would give a demand dominated employment decision, although not in the depressive sense discussed earlier. The causality path through the block diagram from N to W_R would still be reversed, however, and the real wage would still be determined by the supply function. With the supply function moderately inelastic with respect to the real wage even a small additional increase in output tends to lead to further upward pressure on wages and, with marginal productivity declining rapidly, to downward pressure on profits. The tendency to operate above the profit maximising output level follows from three causes. The first is a definition of full employment that requires that unemployment be minimised in order to achieve a low target figure of unemployment. The level of *employment* which this implies could not possibly be justified in terms of the labour demand function which is a representation of the expected marginal product and is derived from the production function. Insistence on this high level of employment creates a sellers' market for labour services just as surely as a genuine demand based on an expected profitable return. The second cause of the

Fig. 7.1 Inflation and levels of social aspiration

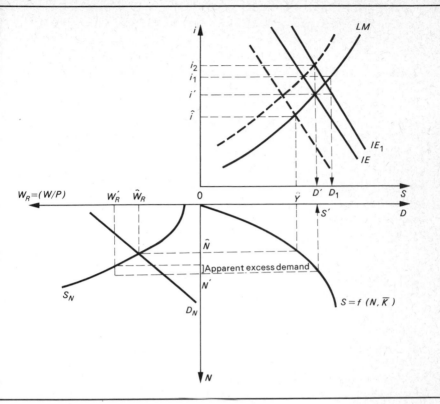

high operating level is the lavish expectations which awareness of standards enjoyed elsewhere and the activities of the communications media tend to induce amongst workers. These tend to become political target standards and so set an output level which government will support and possibly subsidise. These two influences tend to establish the operating point on the production function, and this is shown in the second $IE-LM$ diagram, Fig. 7.1, by N' and S'. The third cause, which completes the 'lock-in' to the labour market pathology is the depressed production function, which reflects low labour productivity, and shows the relatively large amount of labour which is needed to produce the flow of goods and services required by the sanctioned aspiration levels. Profit maximising management would no doubt cut back output and employment, but not only do other objectives become important in large oligopolistic institutions, but in the United Kingdom social, governmental and trade union pressures unite to prevent this. An ironic aspect of the situation is that in times of depression survival

forces firms to try to maximise profit and sometimes this can prove harmful, whereas in times of buoyant demand, when profit maximisation might
save the day, the required pressures are absent.

Having set the scene, it is not difficult to see how inflationary tendencies
build up, assisted by both market forces and by the actions and policies of
government and business. High real-wage levels combined with high levels
of employment produce a large value for employment incomes (high
N' . W_R) and so generate increased consumption in the way described in
the earlier analysis (a way endorsed by Keynes in the *General Theory*,
incidentally). In Fig. 7.1, this moves the *IE* curve to the right establishing
a new aggregate demand level at D_1. The position shown takes into account
the lagged effect of interest rates on investment, so that initially the higher
level of aggregate demand gives a very high interest rate (i_1) but not a
corresponding reduction in investment. Subsequently, investment expenditure plans will be cut back and if there were no other changes, a fresh
income—expenditure equilibrium would be reached at D_2. Long before this
happens, excess demand will have set off an increase in prices; the inflationary process will be under way. As prices rise, there will be two almost
immediate effects, real wages and the effective money supply will be
reduced. The second of these effects, shown by the dotted *LM* curve in the
diagram, will lead to even higher interest rates (i_2) but may be nullified if
the money supply is allowed to increase. As soon as real wages begin to
decline, there will be pressure from the unions to increase money wages at
least to a level that will restore their old purchasing power. A likely delay
period before this higher wage is secured is about two quarters, but when
business does have to pay the new rates it will respond with an almost
immediate price increase in order to maintain profits which, it will be
recalled, were not at a very high level. The subsequent course of events will
depend on the government's reaction to the situation, on the balance
between fiscal and monetary policy and on the timing of the measures
taken. If the will to apply sufficiently firm policies is there, the excess
demand can be eliminated but the process of controlling inflation will need
delicate handling since the high interest rates in the early stages will have
resulted in the cancellation or postponement of investment expenditures.
If these revisions of investment plans result in actual expenditure cuts after
a delay of several quarters they may hit aggregate demand at the same time
as the government's deflationary measures and inflation will be cured only
at the price of severe unemployment.

7.4 Non-Keynesian inflation

It is not our purpose here to review every possible sequence of events that
might lead to or be involved in inflation, but merely to compare the

performance of different models in explaining events known to occur in the real and observable world. Even in this aim, only a few key features of the models can be examined but it is already clear that the standard Keynesian model has only a restricted capacity for analysing inflationary situations. In the sequence sketched in above the elimination of excess demand may not halt the increase in prices, although deflation that produced excess supply probably would do so. Inflation which is not associated with excess demand at or near capacity output cannot be handled by Keynesian models.

The classical models, including general equilibrium models, are also restricted in their ability to handle inflation. In all the classical approaches, changes in the price level are associated with increases or decreases in the money supply. This, it will be remembered, is consistent with the general equilibrium models discussed in earlier chapters and with Patinkin's presentation of the relationship between goods and money markets. The control of inflation, in this view, can be achieved by regulating the money supply. In a simple form, the connexion between money income and the quantity of money in the system can be expressed as

$$Y = k \, \frac{M}{P} \qquad\qquad [7.1]$$

where Y is real income, P the price level, M the quantity of money and k a constant. In the classical scheme, which with appropriate assumptions, can be traced through the block diagrams or the split-axis diagram, the labour market equilibrium determines employment and, through the production function, real income (Y). With M under control and k given, any tendencies for the price level to increase at an undesirably rapid rate can be checked by reducing the money supply. If relative prices and the real wage can all move freely, this should not result in unemployment and a new general equilibrium should result. The constant k in [7.1] represents the velocity of circulation of money since it can readily be seen to be equal to the value of money income divided by the money in the system. Whether this is really a constant or is stable at all in any useful sense is a matter of doubt since it must depend on the reactions and expectations of transactors within the system. It is also doubtful whether the money supply can be controlled with the accuracy and precision that its use as the major weapon against inflation would require, particularly having regard to the lags which are known to exist in this part of the system.

The problem of controlling inflation is complicated by the existence of monopoly and trade union power. The presence of monopoly power does not imply the existence of a total or pure monopoly in any market, but merely the possession by sellers of the power to vary their prices to some degree independently of market forces. For such firms their prices are policy decisions arrived at with the objective of increasing profits (or revenues) or in response to more complex motivations. Similarly the more powerful unions are able to set and to achieve money wage targets. The result of prices and wages being decided as a result of conscious policies rather than as responses to market conditions is that wages and prices may both increase even when there is no excess demand in the market for goods and services. Autonomous price and wage increases are responses to each other and while the evidence is that there is a longer lag in the response of wages to price changes than in the reverse effect, the overall result is to leave employment and real wages unchanged. Exogenous changes such as increases in the prices of imported materials may set the process going, but once it is in motion it will be hard to stop as each set of decision makers tries to maintain their previous position. The long process of tracking effects through the system is omitted, but the effects on expenditure, the cancelling of emergent excess demand by price increases and the signals from profit fluctuations may be readily understood.

Just as inflation may occur when there is no excess demand, excess demand may be present when the system is operating at outputs below capacity. So long as the attempted real expenditure rate is in excess of the rate of supply of goods and services this may occur with consequent pressure on prices, quite without regard to the absolute levels of activity just as the previous process of autonomous wage and price inflation could occur without there being full employment. Again, scenarios are best left for occasions when there is space for a detailed analysis.

7.5 Understanding and prediction

A minimum amount of essential evidence was briefly reviewed earlier in this chapter. The question arises of whether it is necessary at all to build complicated general models. There are a number of two-equation models which relate wages and prices, as jointly determined variables, to other factors. Would not an understanding of inflation be better attempted through such models and through investigations designed to improve our estimates of the parameters of the equations? Using techniques which have now become fairly standard, principally variants and extensions of multiple regression analysis, it is not too difficult to devise equations for all the major components of national income and to combine them in large computable models. The objectives of such models are not so much the understanding, in depth, of macro-economic processes but the prediction of future states of the economy, including states brought about by variations in policy. It may be assumed that the performance of such models will improve in the near future, and perhaps dramatically as improvements are made in computing machinery and in the technical skills processed by economists. If we have the promise of effective computable models, why should we worry about alternative models of fundamental economic processes when it is the outcome of policies that really matters?

There seem to be several reasons why it is still necessary to persist with the attempt to understand macro-economic processes in detail. One reason is that computable models still fall short of the more optimistic promises. On the whole computer experts are more sanguine about such developments than the econometricians who would have to construct such models. Another is that the best models, giving the most accurate predictions, have tended to be partial ones that could, for instance, predict gross domestic product but include no monetary sector. Not only will the model's utility be very limited as soon as policies are envisaged which cannot be incorporated into its structure, but it will be quite unable to act as a device for stimulating thought about new policy combinations. Reliance upon computable models is likely to be an influence towards intellectual conservatism. Yet another reason for continuing to think about the essential nature of economic behaviour and the aggregate effects to which it gives rise is that at any one moment of time, the performance of computable models is assessed against series of past observations. Such series embody not purely economic effects, but economic effects influenced and distorted by government policy. Whatever distortions, and some of them may have been socially beneficial, have been introduced will continue while the same type of policy or combination of policies continues to be applied. Should quite different policies come into popularity, it is not likely that all the equations in the model will continue to predict well. In the same way, the closeness of the fit with past observations, while acting as an assurance of good predictions while social structures and behaviour patterns remain stable will result in errors in prediction when social conditions change.

None of this is meant to denigrate computable models, nor to suggest that econometric research into causative factors in particular sectors of the economy is not valuable or represents a misapplication of academic resources. All these things are necessary and are an integral part of the macro-economic inquiries with which we have been concerned. They impinge upon matters of theory in two ways. Firstly, they suggest some of the forms that the connecting functions might take and secondly they provide a means of testing specific hypotheses that emerge from the major theoretical schemes.

7.6 The acceptance of hypotheses in economic science
The situation which we have been exploring, in which two or more hypotheses give almost equally credible explanations of some sets of events

while they are all less successful in others is not an unusual one in economics or in any other science. By some balance of probabilities, some of which may be very personal, some one explanation must be selected as the preferred hypothesis and as Thomas Kuhn and others have pointed out, even the existence of evidence incompatible with major theoretical schemes will not result in their rejection unless a successor theory is available. One way around the problem of choosing between competing hypotheses is to decide that the preferred one should be the simplest that accounts for the observations. This will not be a very elaborate one with the fullest and most realistic set of assumptions and, at least on one view, an attempt to devise a realistic theory would be misguided. As Professor Friedman has put it

> Truly important and significant hypotheses will be found to have 'assumptions' that are wildly inaccurate descriptive representations of reality and, in general, the more significant the theory, the more unrealistic the assumptions . . . . The reason is simple. A hypothesis is important if it 'explains' much by little, that is, if it abstracts the common and crucial elements from the mass of detailed circumstances . . . .[3]

There is much to respect in this view; it has a venerable ancestry and has been effective in the physical sciences. If simple theories do account for the phenomena observed, there is no need to bring in complicating factors and unnecessary assumptions built in to the theory can only obscure the more direct causation and may be a barrier to development. Milton Friedman's own approach to macro-economic phenomena exemplifies the doctrine stated above very well. The phenomena to be explained and predicted are variations in (nominal) national income and the dominant cause of these fluctuations in the quantity of money in the economic system. Friedman's method was to take an extended and more sophisticated form of Keynes's liquidity preference function and to treat it as a demand function for money. With very simple assumptions about the nature of this function, it is possible to show a correspondence with the older quantity theory. While the empirical evidence in support of this new and more flexible quantity theory is not beyond discussion, the considerable influence of Friedman's work raises strongly the question of whether the attention given to very elaborate macro-economic models is well directed. The question is similar to that considered earlier. If either simple models or rugged but not entirely consistent models predict adequately why bother with complexity or subtlety? A good theory is one which predicts well, is capable of being tested and has not been refuted. It is not enough to reject the new quantity theory or any other simple hypothesis about the determination of national income merely because it does not seem intellectually satisfying. This would be an unscientific and self-indulgent way of dealing with the problem of the acceptance or rejection of hypotheses.

If we are concerned with the control of the economy as well as with the single question of income determination, there is a stronger reason for *not* accepting a very simple hypothesis as the preferred one. Unless employment, interest rates, price movements and real income, as well as money income, are all highly (although not necessarily positively) correlated a theory that furnishes only a single policy instrument, variation in the money supply, will be inadequate for the analysis of policies designed to regulate these other important elements of the economic system. Devoted monetarists would protest at this point in the argument that it is just such attempts at detailed tampering which have proved so disastrously destabilising in the past. For the monetarists, the economy is rather like a very well designed aeroplane which is inherently stable in flight. Once it is on course and flying straight and level, the best thing to do is to leave the controls alone as much as possible. If the economy is to grow at a modest pace, with production expanding year by year, the appropriate policy is to permit a gentle increase in the money supply to keep in step with the increase in output. This would require steady nerves on the part of policy makers to wait, possibly through periods of quite high unemployment, while abberations in the level of economic activity corrected themselves. Even if the delays in response which would follow reliance on monetary policy, in this sense, were politically acceptable, surely some more detailed model is needed in order to track the side effects of monetary policy as they are reflected through the economy and to forecast where action in mitigation of them is likely to be required.

Notes and references

1. Excess capacity and its effect on investment in the United Kingdom economy have been investigated by P. N. Junankar (*Economica*, August, 1970) and by J. P. Burman (*The Econometric Model of the United Kingdom*, Macmillan, 1970) amongst others.

2. 'Money illusion': the illusion that because money income has increased real income must also be greater. In the context of the economic models under discussion, a consumption function expressed in money terms which contributed to aggregate demand in excess of aggregate supply would tend to overstate real consumption expenditures (see Dasgupta and Hagger, *The Objectives of Macro-economic Policy*, Macmillan, 1971).

3. Milton Friedman, 'The methodology of positive economics' in *Essays in Positive Economics*, University of Chicago, 1953.

8
Policy and growth

8.1 The transition to a system in motion

The criticisms of orthodox classical and Keynesian models and the responses which they have evoked in defence of a more modern and sensitive interpretation of the Keynesian system have shaken old certainties and this has had great benefits. It is no longer heresy, or the mark of die-hard conservatism, to question the Keynesian assumptions and the way is open to consider systems which are not classical and yet which can embody a measure of price flexibility. The introduction of information flows and the responses to them has begun to bring macro-economic theory into line with work in other fields and to provide a link with micro-economics. The need to pay attention to the perception, or non-perception, of the signals emitted by trading conditions and the possibility of varying reactions to them has reintroduced the decision maker at macro-economic level as more than a stereotype economic man. While all this holds out new possibilities for the understanding, and therefore control, of macro-economic processes, much work is still oriented towards static equilibria, from which events in disequilibrium are taken as deviations. The existence of equilibrating tendencies is an essential part of economic theory, of course, and without this concept economic events appear as little more than a sequence of random occurrences. The trouble is that the equilibrium position is not a static but a moving one. In the short period, this may not be important and in the areas in which we have been working awareness of each equilibrium position as one point in a dynamic sequence has made it possible to use only slightly modified versions of the comparative-static diagrams. In relating models to policy, however, it is necessary to do more than this; economic growth is a major policy objective, low growth rates restrict the possibilities of improving welfare and the experience of economic growth affects the aspiration levels of wage earners and businessmen.

8.2 Investment and productivity

In all the short-run models which we have considered, investment outlays have been a significant element of total expenditures. Investment expenditures, as we have seen, generate incomes but this is not their only, or their main, function. Net investment outlays, that is outlays on additional, not replacement, equipment, represent increases in the total productive capacity of the economy. Even this is not the end of the matter. The replacement of old equipment by new almost always brings improved techniques to industry, so that both net and gross investment act as vehicles for the transmission of technological change. None of this has been shown in our short-run models and yet it is one of the most significant parts of our economic experience and one which has great impact on the lives of ordinary people. Even in economies such as that of the United Kingdom, where investment outlays are considered to have been low for many years, expenditures on new or replacement equipment run at about 10 per cent of national income, so that the stock of capital equipment grows more quickly than the working population.[1] The result is that with more equipment per worker labour productivity will rise from year to year. This rise in output per worker is not due solely to technical improvements which are associated with the equipment itself, but also to improvements in working methods which may or may not be stimulated by the installation or availability of new machines.

The assumption made in the split-axis diagrams, as in most other short-run analyses, is that the additions made to equipment during the period are too small to affect the production function, which can therefore be considered as dependent on the labour input alone. For comparative short-period analysis, the fundamental causes of the increase in labour productivity need not be of immediate concern; all that is necessary is to see that the production function will undergo a gradual and continuing lift from period to period. This effect is illustrated in Fig. 8.1, where employment and production sub-systems of the economy are shown in vertical form. The change in output per worker is shown by the raised production function, labelled with the capital F, from which it can be seen that a greater total production (aggregate supply, S) can be achieved at every possible level of employment. As the production function lifts, the demand curve for labour moves outwards showing the increased *marginal* productivity of labour. Naturally, the equilibrium output level and the optimum employment level ($\hat{N}$) also increase, as does the equilibrium real wage. If circumstances do exist in which there is false excess demand for labour, with consequent upward pressure on both real and money wages, as one of the models discussed in the last chapter suggests, the most effective cure would seem to be found in increasing labour productivity

Fig. 8.1   Output and labour productivity

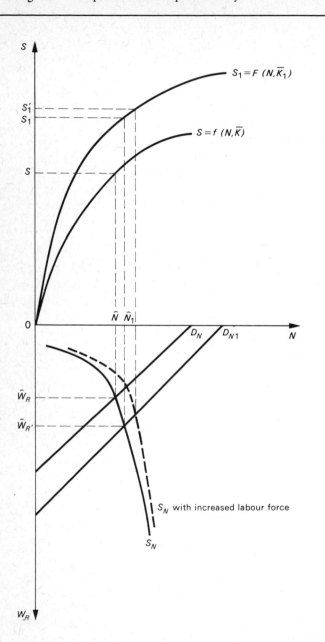

fast enough for the aspiration and employment levels dictated by social and social goals to become the equilibrium economic ones. It goes without saying, that social goals, in so far as they concern material standards are also dynamic so that the problem is one of ensuring that the production function moves upwards fast enough to ensure that full employment output can meet the social target and yet still be profitable.

8.3 The growth path of the economy

Although economic models intended primarily for short-run analysis have tended to make only the most formal of gestures towards the correspondence principle and the underlying dynamic situation, the construction of long-run models has drawn heavily on the conditions for short-run Keynesian equilibrium. Since, as we have seen, Keynesian equilibria tend to develop in demand dominated situations of decline in which wage and price flexibilities are insufficient to reconcile expenditure plans and output levels, it is not surprising that models based on them do not provide for factor substitution in response to changing factor prices. The best known models of this type are the ones developed independently by R. Harrod (now Sir Roy Harrod) and E. Domar[2] in the days when the Keynesian analysis was still 'the new economics'. It was natural then to be concerned with the possibility of a growth path which still left resources, especially labour, under employed. This was Domar's starting point and it is a suitable one from which to pick up the threads of our earlier analysis. Essentially what Domar noticed was the discrepancy between the increasing productive capacity, shown in the previous section of this chapter by the steadily rising production function and the static level of aggregate demand given by the Keynesian equilibrium. Even if aggregate demand were brought to the full employment level, the equilibrium level of investment expenditures would provide growing output capacity, a situation which would lead to under-utilised equipment and unemployed labour. This effect could be avoided if investment expenditures were large enough for their effects on aggregate demand, when amplified through the multiplier, to equal the increased capacity. The growth path along which capacity and demand are in equilibrium is calculated, in the Harrod—Domar models, by assuming a fixed link (the output/capital ratio) between additions to output and the investment outlays which make them possible. This equilibrium growth path, as is well known, turns out to be an exponential path given by

$$Y = Y_0 e^{\rho t} \qquad\qquad [8.1]$$

where Y is the level of income, e is the exponential constant, ρ is a growth rate equal to the product of the marginal propensity to consume and the output/capital ratio and t is the time elapsed since some initial point at which income was equal to Y_0. In non-mathematical terms this gives a growth path along which national income and national product increase at a constant percentage rate each period, so that the path grows steeper year by year as the *absolute* value of the percentage increases becomes larger. Harrod's versions of the model contrast this 'warranted' rate, which would give zero excess demand in the goods market, with a 'natural' rate determined by the growth of the labour force. The warranted growth rate is given by the ratio of savings to income (denoted by the symbol s) divided by the capital/output ratio (v), which is the reciprocal of the output/capital ratio used by Domar. If the idea of the natural rate is extended to include both the growth rate of working population (n) and the growth rate of labour productivity (p) the full employment growth rate that does not generate excess demand, ignoring bottleneck effects would have to satisfy the condition

$$\frac{s}{v} = n + p \qquad\qquad [8.2]$$

This requirement carries the assumption that the proportion of labour to capital in the production process is fixed. If this assumption is relaxed and the capital/labour ratio is permitted to vary with factor prices, or more accurately with real factor rewards, there will be tendencies at work which will alter the capital/output ratio and so bring the warranted and natural rates together. This would give a neo-classical model which would be supply dominated and would not produce a 'knife-edged' growth path which was constantly threatened by explosive breakaway or catastrophic decline. Models of this sort began to be developed from the mid-1950s onwards as did other, counter-classical, alternatives concerned with the effect of income distribution on the savings ratio and yet others concerned with the relationship between productivity and other factors. Meanwhile, the Cambridge criticisms of aggregate production functions, formally irrefutable but not necessarily so destructive in practical terms, continued.

Much of this review of simple growth theory may be very familiar, but it is the minimum which is needed in order to put previous work into an appropriate context. We may now accept the concept of an equilibrium growth path and perhaps, as well, the idea that there are forces at work which, in the long run, prevent the wide divergence of the natural and warranted rates of growth.

8.4 Growth and the model
Once the idea of an equilibrium growth path is accepted as part of our analytical equipment, it is not difficult to relate it to the general model set

out in earlier chapters and to the ideas about investment and productivity discussed in section 8.2. As the working population increases, the supply curve begins to move out along the N-axis, with more labour being offered at each real wage. At the same time, increases in labour productivity are raising the production function in the way illustrated in Fig. 8.1. This, with the connexion between the demand for labour and the production function, means that both demand and supply curves in the labour market are changing. As the equilibrium employment level increases, the total output in real terms, represented on the S-axis in the diagram also grows. Reverting to the split-axis diagrams used in earlier chapters, we could imagine this moving the lower, aggregate supply arrow, steadily along the S-axis while parallel increases in aggregate demand, due to the investment expenditures and the multiplier process, kept the upper arrow exactly in pace with it as the economy moved along the growth path. Small deviations between the two arrows (minor appearances of excess demand or excess supply) might be dealt with by classical adjustments so long as entre-preneurs' expectations and consumers' expenditure plans remained substantially unchanged, but larger deviations would set in motion one of the non-classical processes discussed in Chapters 6 and 7. In the very long run, too, response to changing factor prices might lead to gradual move-ments in the ratio in which the factors of production were employed. With the classical influences confined to small-scale deviations and to very long-run effects, other pressures must be at work to keep natural and warranted rates of growth together in the areas and over the time spans with which we are mainly concerned. These other influences would, in practice, include not only the purely economic effects with which most growth models are concerned, but also government policies. This has, as one result, the possibility that aggregate demand may exceed the rate of output dominated aggregate supply. This may be visualised as the demand arrow pulling ahead of the S-arrow after an autonomous increase in government expenditure that has shifted the IE-curve to the right. If output is near to capacity, as it will have been if the economy was previously on its equi-librium path, prices should increase to eliminate the excess of expenditure planned. If they do not move quite quickly enough, strong signals will come in to businessmen that additional profits are still to be made. There will be such rapid sales that some goods become in short supply and while further price increases will be one response another will be to organise imported substitutes as quickly as possible. The gap between aggregate supply from the home economy and aggregate demand will therefore be met partly by increasing prices, which will reduce demand in terms of real claims on goods and services, and partly by imports. On the demand side, it will be recalled, expenditure on imports represents a withdrawal.

8.5 The United Kingdom growth experience

Having begun to open the closed economy model to the outside world, with imports becoming part of the analysis, it is tempting to see whether the statistical series reinforce or immediately refute the position taken. So far as the model of the economy is concerned it would be necessary to make some assumptions about exports. The appropriate one seems to be that exports grow quite independently of the home economy except that the overall growth trend of exports will be aided or retarded by the price of export goods. Similarly the prices of imported goods in relation to those of home produced goods would reinforce or negate the influences outlined in the previous section. Translated into everyday experience, a model structured in the way suggested would give a long-run growth path along which output increased at a constant percentage rate year by year. Because of government expenditures, and possibly other factors, the expenditure path would tend to overshoot the long-run output path from time to time and this would lead to balance of payments problems. Subsequent corrective action by government would be likely to push actual performance well below the growth path, particularly if delayed monetary effects were felt at the same time. The next period of recovery and increased growth might proceed at a faster rate since there would be a reserve of capacity and would in due course be corrected once again, leading to the familiar 'stop–go' policy sequence.

An essential stage in comparison with the United Kingdom growth experience is the determination of the long-run growth path. Working with Gross Domestic Product at factor cost and constant 1970 prices and taking into account the indications that the years from 1970 to 1972 were below trend, the appropriate annual rate of growth is 2.8 per cent. The figures for the growth in productivity are entirely consistent with this, with the working population having grown since 1950 at something rather less than one-half of 1 per cent per annum and labour productivity having increased at an average rate of 2.7 per cent. This consistency between the two sets of figures is largely a matter of arithmetic, of course, but at least it gives a clearer impression of the nature of the growth on the supply side. With the working population almost constant in size, by far the greatest part of the growth in output must come from increases in labour productivity, whatever the underlying causes of this might be. The 2.8 per cent growth path and the actual observations of Gross Domestic Product are shown in Fig. 8.2. The several occasions on which government policy has pushed the level of activity below the growth path can be seen as can the accelerations as the level of output recovers and breaks through the long-run path again. Below the main diagram are shown the deficits or surpluses on the balance of payments current account. It would be unwise to make very firm

Fig. 8.2　The growth path of the United Kingdom economy

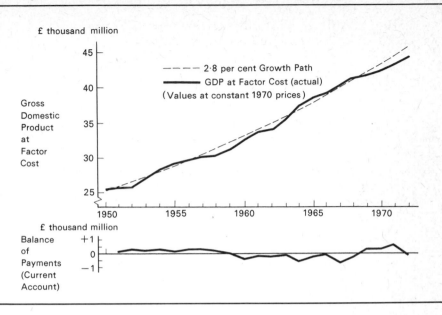

inferences from a comparison of figures of this sort. Exchange rate fluctuations and variations in interest rates were interacting over the whole period and the period includes the devaluation of 1967. However, the general pattern of observations is not inconsistent with the view put forward. It could be added that the periods of rapid growth for which governments have claimed credit at various times are all periods of recovery from below the growth path.

8.6　An extension to policy options

Growth models add a further dimension to our understanding of the influences at work in the economy and the constraints which act upon them. Opening out the analysis to include some aspects of international trading, the ones that form the 'interface' between the domestic economy and the international economic system, further extends the list of influences upon demand and growth. The problem of economic control is revealed as being more complex but the range of policy options is extended. To follow this in more detail, we could add another component to the fine-structure block diagram of Fig. 8.3. The main elements of this addition to the system are, naturally, imports (M) and exports (X) with the difference between these values giving the figure for the balance of payments on current account (B). Imports are shown as dependent on

Fig. 8.3　The impact of overseas trade

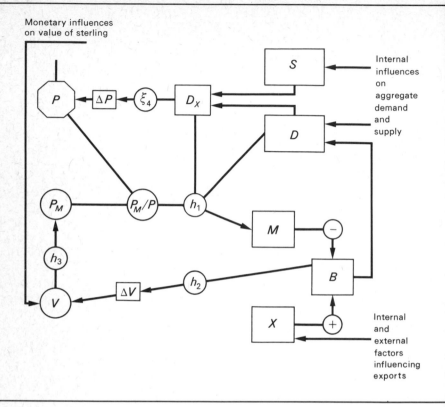

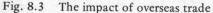

aggregate demand and also on the level of excess demand, whereas exports are taken to depend on the level of world trade. Both imports and exports vary inversely with their prices, shown by the symbols P_X and P_M, although in the case of imports it is not the price alone but the ratio of import prices to domestic prices (P_M/P) which is the appropriate influence. The prices of imports and exports do not depend only on market and cost considerations, which are not shown in the diagram, but also on the rates of exchange between the pound sterling and other currencies. Since these rates tend to move together the value of the pound in terms of other currencies is shown by a single symbol, V. Imports and exports are, respectively, withdrawals from and injections into, the income–expenditure circuit and so connect back to aggregate demand. For the sake of simplicity, no connexions are shown to aggregate supply, which must therefore be taken to represent the net real flow of goods and services offered for sale in the home economy by the productive system. The feedback of imports as a reduction of aggregate demand establishes an import multiplier effect which works against and modifies the main multiplier process.

An acceptable policy mix is usually taken to require the reduction of unemployment to a politically and socially acceptable level and the attainment of a favourable, or not too disastrously negative, balance of payments. The conventional approach to this problem of control is to use net government expenditure to influence aggregate demand and employment and to use monetary policy, through its effect on interest rates, to encourage an inflow of foreign funds sufficient to finance any current account deficit and also to support the value of the pound. The disadvantages of this system in the days when sterling was a major reserve currency are well known; the funds attracted were volatile, the supported pound resulted in export prices that were unduly high and made it even more difficult to solve the current account problem on the balance of payments and so threw even more weight and urgency on to the monetary side. The fragility of the system led, not surprisingly, to speculation against the pound and to eventual devaluation. The emotional commitment to support of the pound led to the savage applications of these policies which can be seen reflected in the growth path diagram. The inception of a system of floating exchange rates should have taken some of the tension out of this problem area, since a poor current account balance would have led, through the ordinary currency transactions required in the course of trade, to a lower value of the pound and so to higher import prices and to lower prices in export markets. The freeing of monetary policy from the necessity of working to attract funds from overseas would allow it to be used more freely in pursuit of internal objectives.

The state of affairs described in this section and relationships between excess demand and the balance of payments such as those outlined in the previous sections have led some influential economists, particularly Professors Kaldor and Nield at Cambridge, to suggest that the conventional application of the two main policy instruments might advantageously be reversed. In Professor Nield's words[3] . . . 'the Budget should be used to determine the foreign balance and the exchange rate to determine the level of activity'. For the second policy instrument, action to restore full employment from a moderate under-employment equilibrium with no excess demand in the goods market would begin with a reduction (however secured) in V (Fig. 8.3). This would tend to increase import prices and to lower export prices, improving the balance of payments by increasing X and reducing M, but since both imports and exports connect back to aggregate demand both injection and withdrawal multiplier processes would be set in motion. The eventual level of demand would be higher than before and the process would be very likely to induce matching increases in aggregate supply so long as credit and liquidity conditions were favourable. The question is whether the increase in activity generated by the fall in the rate of exchange is sufficient to justify its use in this way. The proponents of this approach to economic control contend that it would be, that the eventual state of the balance of payments would not be greatly changed from the initial one and that the main effects would be on demand, output and employment. Critics of the approach point to additional 'leakages' from the expenditure circuit.

The trouble is that experience along the growth path shows that there is an association between changes in aggregate demand and the balance of payments and if this looks like a promising means of control, *another* instrument is needed to regulate the level of activity. Second thoughts, however, may suggest that if monetary policy is the fundamental means of influencing the exchange rate, then the dilemma is a false one and the original problem of finding the right combination of fiscal and monetary policies to secure an acceptable balance of payments and a high level of employment remains. When the instruments are used together it is clear that they will interact with each other through the balance of payments and the multiplier circuits and in other ways.

Notes and references

1. Gross domestic fixed capital formation in the United Kingdom in 1972 was valued at £9,382 million (at 1970 prices) of which £4,468 million represented new or replacement equipment. The net value of the capital stock, excluding buildings and works, was about £52,000 million. Replacement equipment represented about two-thirds of the total investment figure, leaving some £1,400 million for new, that is additional, equipment. This gives a growth rate of approximately 2¾ per cent per annum for the stock of equipment.

2. The most accessible of the original articles are E. Domar, 'Expansion and employment', *Econometrica*, 1947, and R. F. Harrod, 'An essay in dynamic theory', *Economic Journal*, 1939.

3. Letter to *The Times*, 26 February 1974.

9
The dynamics of prices and incomes

9.1 The failure of demand management

The changing nature of our understanding of macro-economic processes, which has been the main concern of this book, has led to an increasing involvement with aspects of human behaviour which are not explicable in purely economic terms. It is possible for the economist to observe such behaviour and to note its economic effects but not, usually, to offer an explanation in terms of the social psychology or social institutions which brought it about. This was the case with the inflation model presented in Chapter 7 (section 7.3) in which rising aspiration levels set high consumption targets and social conventions about the acceptable level of employment combined with revenue-maximising behaviour by business established a high level of GDP with apparent, though definitely not classical, excess demand in the labour market. Treating an inflation of this kind by conventional reductions in aggregate demand is unlikely to be successful unless it is carried through with a ruthlessness that ensures that aggregate demand falls more quickly than aggregate supply. Only by restricting cash flows and the availability of credit to the point at which business becomes responsive to pressures on profits and by letting unemployment grow to a level which damages labour's ambitions for higher living standards can such a policy attain its end. Policy makers who regard the manipulation of aggregate demand as the main weapon against inflation are likely to believe themselves to be employing Keynesian remedies and so to be opposed to the creation of unemployment on the scale required. This is almost a guarantee that such policies, which are in any case neither socially nor politically acceptable when used with the required panache, will not be effective. They are also unacceptable to the trade unions who, as Aubrey Jones has pointed out 'can launch a counter attack on an attempt by government to induce higher unemployment'. Both statements from trade unionists and Mr Jones's testimony suggest that the unions have been developing their own, rather simplistic, model of macro-economic processes:

> Trade union leaders had come to learn that, to the extent that incomes move faster than prices, they could thereby expand consumption, expand demand, and might indeed accelerate the rate of economic growth.[1]

Recourse to the diagrammatic techniques used earlier shows that it is possible to increase aggregate demand in real terms, and that is what matters, by means of aggressive policies to increase money wages only if an increase in W_R, the real wage, leads to an increase in real income from employment $(N \cdot W_R)$, which it may not do, and also to an increase in the propensity to consume, which it may. Unless there is a corresponding increase in supply, the result of the attempt to negate government policy will be more price rises, more bitterness and more militancy. The results of ineffective attempts to cure inflation by demand management seem likely to have the results of stimulating union militancy without curtailing union power. Output is likely to be cut back to some extent as demand falls, but rising wage costs will keep profits under pressure. As envisaged in the earlier discussion, prices and wages will continue to rise even if there is very little, or no, excess demand, but interests within society are likely to become increasingly divergent. Almost inevitably, economic processes give way to political ones and the political consensus is lost as programmes become polarised towards one set of interests or another.

9.2 Productivity and information flows

The information flows which determine aspiration levels tend to be direct and unambiguous although they are not necessarily accurate. Those which affect the level of output are indirect and uncertain. Sometimes links are lost altogether, as with the notional excess demands that provide no signals that would stimulate production. As well as operating at a strictly micro-economic level to influence individual decision makers and at macro-economic level, in their aggregate effects, information flows produce inter-industry effects. Not only do workers in different industries tend to acquire common aspiration levels as the transmission of information through society becomes more rapid and efficient but they also become very aware of the differentials that exist between different sections of industry. The increasing professionalism of trade unions has probably helped this trend as has the publication of more information from official sources. This heightened awareness, totally legitimate in itself, makes the solution of the problem of inflation more difficult since it seems to rule out increases in labour productivity as the remaining conventional solution. With increased productivity the economy would be able to afford a high real wage, meet the social output target and still produce a satisfactory return for industry and business. In the aggregate this seems promising, but technological progress occurs unevenly throughout industry. This means that productivity per worker varies between one industry and another, between manufacturing industry and the service industries and between labour intensive and capital intensive industries. Moreover, the diffusion of new processes through the industrial structure is quite slow and tends to move from science-based industries to more traditional ones.[2] In the industries in which productivity is increasing rapidly, wages tend to increase at about the same pace and this creates differentials between one industry and another. Partly because of unionisation and, increasingly, because workers from many industries are represented within single large unions, these differentials are very well perceived and action is soon taken to correct them. The industries which experience increased productivity are better able to meet wage increases than those which do not do so. These less fortunate industries, which tend to be the traditional and labour intensive ones, find themselves forced to raise prices as wage increases are transmitted to them with the elimination of inter-industry differentials.[3] Since these industries have not experienced the reduction of unit costs due to improvements in technology, their price rises tend to be more rapid than those in the technically advanced sectors of industry. The result of all this is that wages and prices in the economy as a whole would tend to increase more rapidly than labour productivity even if no additional factors at all were involved.

9.3 The circumvention of the labour market

The quite early recognition that demand management did not offer an acceptable solution to the problem of inflation combined with a justified lack of belief that productivity improvements could make more than a long-term contribution, made it necessary to look for some other instrument of policy to control the rate at which prices and wages increased. Of the two obvious approaches one, the control of the money supply, was ruled out because of a long-standing belief in its ineffectiveness which was, in due course, reinforced by the Radcliffe doctrine that the money supply was difficult to define or control and that in any case the velocity of circulation was not only unstable but was probably perverse in its reactions. The other approach was to over-ride market forces in some way and in particular to substitute some process of civilised negotiation or, alternatively, a bureaucratic or even legislative process. Naturally, governments of the left tended to be more enthusiastic about controlling prices and those of the right put greater emphasis on the control of incomes. These attempts, beginning with rather quiet and restrained agreements with the trade union movement during the period of office of the first post-war Labour Government (statutory price controls were still in existence), passed through various institutional arrangements of increasing formality to outright legislation, as in 1966—69 and 1973—74. In order to make these policies effective, since even the implementation of legislation depended on union acquiescence, it was necessary for successive governments to encourage the centralisation and formalisation of negotiations. Agreement depends more and more on the results of high-level meetings between representatives of the trade unions, the government and the employers with orthodox local negotiation left to clear up details and report anomalies. A number of consequences flow from these tendencies, such as the revision of the role of local negotiators and the encouragement of shopfloor militancy, which in turn feeds back to influence policy at higher levels, but our concern is with the effect on the macro-economic system of replacing the labour market with an alternative mechanism. As the detailed workings of this mechanism are too involved for an extended discussion here and since they require other disciplines, in addition to economics, for their explanation, we must regard the alternative process as a 'socio-economic black box', without any explicitly revealed internal structure rather like the block representing the employment sub-system in Fig. 6.1. The temporary supersession of the labour market by another process does not mean that market forces disappear from the system; they may be frustrated or may have effects elsewhere in the economy but they still exist and may eventually disrupt the alternative mechanism. The market process, however, depends on information and expectations and the suggestion is that successive experiments with institutional and legislative control have tended to distort the operation of the labour market so that the rate of change of wage rates is no longer responsive to market conditions.

The effect of labour market conditions on wage rates is usually illustrated by allowing the percentage of unemployment to stand as an indicator of excess supply so that a negative relationship should be observable between unemployment and the percentage rate of change of wages. A. W. Phillips fitted curves to historical data and showed that the expected negative relationship did exist over a long period of time and that it had a statistically regular and stable form. Evidence that incomes policies tended to distort the labour market came from Lipsey and Parkin in results first disclosed in 1969 and published in *Economica* in 1970. These findings were confirmed and strengthened in a further paper published by J. M. Parkin alone a few months later.[4] The essential point of this research is that in periods in which an incomes policy is in operation, the relationship between unemployment and the rate of change of wages is lost, the downward sloping Phillips's curve becoming replaced by an almost horizontal line. Although this work does not indicate permanent damage to the labour market, which seems to come back into action reasonably quickly to restore the expected relationships in 'policy-off' periods, it does show that when incomes policies are applied in periods of even moderate unemployment wages will tend to rise more quickly than they would have done if market forces had been allowed to act on their own. The critical cross-over point at which incomes policies appear to become counterproductive is shown in Fig. 9.1 as occurring at an unemployment level of less than 2 per cent. It appears that the negotiations taking place within the socio-economic black box are likely to increase wage inflation when they are combined with restrictive demand policies designed to secure a withdrawal

Fig. 9.1   Unemployment and wage rates

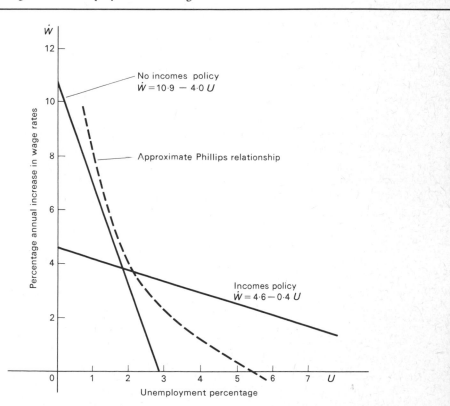

from very high levels of output. It would be better to let the cut-back in demand work on its own.

9.4 Interaction between economic and social systems

In the situation which is reflected in the Lipsey and Parkin equations we are observing the outcome of an interaction between social and economic systems. The actions of participants in the negotiations which precede the announcement of an incomes policy measure, whether it is the result of a consensus or not, are determined by the roles which they are playing, by their own self-images, by their expectations and perceptions of the situation and by their estimates of what is expected of them by colleagues and subordinates. In the analysis of the effects of technological change and increases in labour productivity, social, technical and economic systems are involved and the emulation effect that spreads wages increases through the structure whether or not industries can afford them owes its impetus to notions of equity and fairness that might not have been present in another society or at another time. The dynamics of competitive situations sometimes over-ride human rationality, so that even if a new round of price increases is initiated by rises in the prices of imported commodities, for instance, individual trade unions and individual trade unionists feel compelled to press for higher wages, because to fail to do so would be to be left behind. The individuals are caught in a prisoners' dilemma; if none joined in all would be better off, but to be left out is to be dead.

The increasing importance of centralised wage bargaining and of trade union intervention in the political process in a most powerful way has the result that groups which are not well connected in the negotiations or have no say in the high level power plays come off very badly. The plight of such people is well known; the cases of pensioners, disabled people and some public service employees come to mind. Similarly, the incomes of employees in some of the labour intensive industries that can not, in the nature of things, make great gains in productivity may fail to keep pace with price rises. There are also groups in the middle classes which find themselves without power when inflation is combined with reductions in output and demand. A further development can be envisaged in which the almost horizontal relationship between wage rate increases and unemployment becomes not an occasional but a permanent feature of the economic system. Administered incomes programmes combined with behind the scenes power-bargaining could well lead to the formation of other interest- and action-groups so that each round of price and wage increases is fought both harder and faster lifting the horizontal line higher in each period. There is evidence that this situation contains some of the ingredients for progression from 'normal' inflation to 'strato-inflation'.

It would not be appropriate to advance the argument further here, nor to give way to the temptation to build models in fields other than economics, but at some time the attempt to combine econometric and sociological studies in a new analysis of non-Keynesian inflation must be made.

9.5 Does inflation matter?

The answer that emerges from the foregoing must be that inflation does matter. It may be true, as a very distinguished economist has recently written, that the view emerging from the *General Theory* is that, broadly, it does not. This answer from the illustrious dead, appropriate to other circumstances and to another time cannot be definitive. When inflation becomes socially divisive during a period of almost stationary real income, the Marxian prophesies of capitalism destroyed by its internal contradictions seem capable of being fulfilled.

Notes and references

1. Aubrey Jones, *The New Inflation: The Politics of Prices and Incomes*, Andre Deutsch, 1973, p. 37.

2. See R. E. Johnston, 'Technical progress and innovation', *Oxford Economic Papers*, July 1966.

3. See D. Jackson and H. A. Turner in *Do Trade Unions Cause Inflation?*, Department of Applied Economics Occasional Paper number 36, C.U.P., 1972; and H. A. Turner's final note in the same volume.

4. These two papers are 'Incomes policy: a re-appraisal' by R. G. Lipsey and J. M. Parkin in *Economica*, May 1970; and J. M. Parkin, 'Incomes policy: some further results on the determination of the rate of change of money wages', November 1970 in the same journal. The Phillips' paper is 'Unemployment and wage rates', *Economica*, 1958.

10

Problems of economic control

10.1 The system to be controlled

This book began with a discussion of the relationship between government policy and economic theory and it is fitting that having made revisions to the basic macro-economic model, we should return to make a new appraisal of economic policy and of the methods and objectives of economic control. The revisions to the basic model were not made capriciously but followed, almost inevitably, from the criticisms of Keynesian theory and the reactions of economists who were unable to swallow the neo-classical alternative. The outcome of the long debate between Keynesian and neo-classical economists was not the discarding of one system in favour of the other but the realisation that both shared a common structure. With the change of emphasis in the debate, neither classical nor Keynesian reactions are ruled out in themselves, but the introduction of income-constrained processes and reactions to information flows, which are imperfect and liable to distortion, makes the classical self-adjustment doubtful unless deviations from general equilibrium are small. This does not mean that equilibrating tendencies are absent, but the transfer of attention to the dynamic situation makes it clear that the equilibrium is a moving one. What we have is an equilibrium long-run growth path about which there occur cyclical, or quasi-cyclical, deviations which are largely policy induced. The system to be controlled is an economic one, but events in adjacent systems, which form the parts of the total environment in which the national economy exists and functions, constantly jolt and nudge the economy off its long-run path. When these disturbances, or some internal cause, set the economy on a decline from its growth path, the strong inference to be drawn from the earlier analysis is that its behaviour becomes demand-dominated. Aggregate supply adjusts quickly to reductions in aggregate demand because decisions are income- and liquidity-constrained and these constraints may apply to firms as well as to consumers. This is one case of a constrained response to a changing situation and from the point of view of the theory of control, we can see that the existence of the constraints gives pattern to the observed behaviour and makes it more predictable. While, in this situation, the constraints make action to correct the deviation from desired output and employment necessary, they also help to make the decision about the required action easier. Constraints make response to change less variable and less random; they reduce the 'variety' in the system.[1] In a recession we know that the reactions of producers are inhibited by information failures as well as by the more direct constraints and there are information constraints in the recovery process, too. As the economy climbs back towards the equilibrium path businessmen find their actions both information- and capacity-constrained. In the early stages of recovery, there will be excess capacity and supply and demand are likely to move up together but as the ascent goes on this will be used up and there will also be uncertainty about the length of time for which the improvement in trade will continue. If this is so, we should expect to find excess demand emerging in the later stages of a recovery, resulting in an acceleration of prices as aggregate supply becomes constrained by capacity considerations. In terms of ex-post observations of real, or price corrected, magnitudes, this appears as a price acceleration combined with a deceleration of the growth of gross domestic product.

The behaviour of businessmen and consumers in this last set of circumstances underlines the importance of expectations in economic processes. As can be seen from the growth path diagram in Fig. 8.2, the recovery periods tended, until the mid-1960s, to last for two or three years so that there was time for expectations of continued prosperity to develop. Rather in line with Friedman's permanent income hypothesis for consumption and the Eisner investment theories, expenditure plans would tend to be revised in accordance with these changed expectations. The longer lags before investment plans are able to be implemented contribute to the situation described. Events within the economic system both affect and are affected by changes in expectation and some of these interactions have cumulative effects so that repeated frustration of expectations, as recoveries are curtailed to protect the balance of payments, for instance, may cause downward revisions of plans that influence the course of subsequent economic and policy cycles. The system over which a measure of control is attempted, and is expected, is a very open one in ways other than the obvious one of being exposed to events overseas.

10.2 Concepts in the control of socio-economic systems

One function of macro-economic models is to display the structure of an economy, another is to permit the drawing of accurate boundaries of the system over which control is attempted. Since the system *is* an open one, this involves the isolation of some features of economic life from the whole confused mass of events as they are actually experienced. Failure to recognise the intentional elimination of many non-economic influences leads to the naive discontents that economics does not correspond to the 'real world'. An alternative is to draw the boundaries of the system a little wider and there have recently been movements in this direction. Since we are here concerned with problems of control, there are some very apparent dangers in widening the boundaries of the system to be controlled, since the measure of social and psychological control which is acceptable in a democratic society is limited. The more realistic course, for the present and, one hopes, for a very long time, is to regard the economic effects of social disturbances as problems of interaction between the economic system and other parts of society. These interface problems, trade union militancy is an example, may then be dealt with in ways appropriate to that part of the whole macro-system to which they properly belong. It goes without saying that model building is not definitive in any final sense and that alternative demarcations of system boundaries can, and should, be tried in order to predict the probable outcomes of more extensive schemes of control.

The nature of economic control can be seen if the situation is displayed as a schematic diagram:

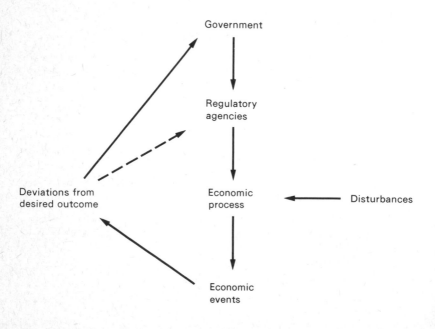

Responsibility for devising policies and translating them into commands rests with the government, but these commands are made effective and implemented in detail by various *regulatory agencies*, the civil service and the monetary authorities. The actions of these agencies impinge on the *economic process*, the ongoing interaction between producers, consumers and their stocks of assets, with all the exchanges that this involves, which has been the subject of our modelling ventures. The result of the workings of the economic process as influenced by the regulatory agencies is a succession of *economic events*, but these events also reflect disturbances of various kinds that have also modified the outcome of the economic process. The economic events as experienced will inevitably differ from those intended by the government and so when deviations from the desired outcomes are reported to the government or to its regulatory agencies policies and the implementation of them can be modified. It is not difficult to see that if reporting to government or its agencies is slow (the main link is shown to government where responsibility primarily lies, with a supporting one to the regulatory agencies) a series of administrative lags will have to be superimposed on those known to exist within the economic system itself. The distortions superimposed by inaccurate reporting of deviations do not need emphasis. If the boundaries of the economic process itself are drawn too widely, it will appear to be generating its own disturbances so that control will seem to be even more difficult if it is conducted as if the system were predictable in its response. This puts the earlier remarks on system boundaries into perspective.

The link from the observed sequence of events back to the regulatory agencies and to government is, of course, a feedback loop of a kind which is very common in many control systems and is well discussed in the literature of cybernetics as are the effects of sluggish or, alternatively, over-sensitive, regulators. The analogies in economic control are obvious.

Even when the economic system is defined in the most suitable way for control purposes, it will still produce a variety of response, both because of its internal operations and as a result of shocks from outside. The principle to be invoked here is that the controller-regulator must be able to display as much variety in regulation as the system does in its aberrations from the course planned for it. An analogy here might be with the cowman who needs a boy and a dog to control the lateral wandering of his herd to left and right while his shouts from behind keep it travelling in the right direction. The government and its agencies require as many distinct instruments as the economic system has ways of deviating from the multi-dimensional path laid out for it by current policy. In the usual terminology this is expressed by saying that the government requires as many instruments as policy targets. The principle is of wider application than this, however, and variation must be matched over time and in the manner of deviation from prescribed targets, for example in the rapidity with which incomes grow or decline, in the magnitude of the deviation and in the total effect of the deviation up to a certain point in time.[2]

10.3 The objectives of economic policy

The basic neo-classical and the orthodox Keynesian visions of the forces which govern economic events are still the principal sources of economic insight at the political level in spite of the misgivings which individual politicians may have about their validity. It is true that there is a growing band of agnostics who do not claim to know what is going on but are sure that they can deal with events if they are given the chance, but even this group is forced to choose its main instruments of policy from the array devised by others with firmer ideas about the relationships involved. There are also rather more people in, and on the fringes of, political life who take a monetarist position and most of these would align themselves with colleagues who retain faith in the market system. Although these several groups disagree about the remedies which should be applied, there is virtually total agreement about the objectives at which they should aim. A generally acceptable list of policy objectives would certainly include

a high level of employment,
a satisfactory rate of growth,
reasonable stability of the internal price level,
a favourable balance of payments

and also a 'welfare' objective embodying views about the distribution of incomes, the degree of support given to the dependent population and similar matters. Although the relative importance of these objectives might differ between groups having different social and economic philosophies, so that those to the left of centre could be expected to give higher priority to the full employment and welfare objectives, these differences of emphasis would be less important when the parties were in office. Another point of difference that ought to be discernible would concern the degree of willingness to intervene in the economy. This has been detectable in the earlier years of Conservative administrations, when they have initiated policies such as the withdrawal of investment grants and the reduction of support for 'lame duck' industries, but the return to interventionist policies seems to have been even more vigorous when the inevitable economic crises has occurred. There is some truth in the dictum that 'we are all Keynesians now' in the sense that the overtones and apparatus of policy are Keynesian; it seems even more the case that we are all pragmatists now whenever real emergencies have to be faced. Another common feature of governments' attitudes towards economic control is the tendency to accept responsibility for the attainment of all five objectives but to concentrate on one, or at the most, two when in office. This, too, is unsurprising, for there are inter-dependencies between the objectives which prevent their fulfilment to an equal degree. It follows that as soon as one objective becomes of over-riding importance the other competing, member of an interdependent pair must be temporarily abandoned. Two of these interdependencies between objectives have been explored in a certain amount of detail in an earlier analysis, these are the relationship between the rate of change of prices and the level of unemployment and that between the level of economic activity and the balance of payments. Earlier in this chapter, too, we have seen a relationship between deviations from the growth path and changes in the price level. Although our analysis indicated slightly more subtle interpreta-tion this is often discussed as a straight trade-off between growth and price stability.

The difficulties of economic control are exacerbated by the fact that there are dependencies between the major policy instruments as well as between objectives. The most important of these interlinks the operation of fiscal and monetary policies and so casts doubt on the whole basis of economic control. The source of this confusion is the increasing tendency for government expenditure to outrun taxation so that a very large budget deficit must be covered by borrowing. When these borrowed funds come from the general public, all is well but if they are obtained from the banking system by means of sales of Treasury Bills, an increase in the supply of money is bound to follow. This is because the acquisition of these short-term securities enlarges the asset base on which the banks' power to create credit depends. For technical reasons, this method of borrowing tends to be more popular than the issuing of long-dated stocks and in spite of determined attempts to reduce government expenditure, the money supply has tended to expand, although the rate of increase is beginning to decline. It will be realised that the triming of public sector expenditure in order to reduce the borrowing requirement prevents the attainment of welfare objectives as standards decline in health services, education and other amenities.

10.4 Control and the model

Something of the complexity of the control problem can be seen from the extended version of the adapted comparative static diagram in Fig. 10.2. Here, as before, it must be remembered that each static position is merely a reflection of an underlying dynamic process and to emphasise this the policy diagram is preceded by a smoothed version of the deviations of the UK economy from its growth path (Fig. 10.1). This should not be taken to

Fig. 10.1   Deviations from the growth path

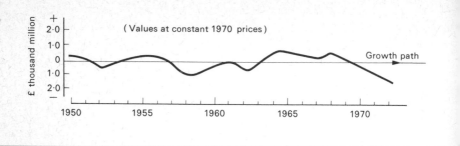

imply that the policy diagram is applicable only to British conditions but merely that it cannot be read apart from its corresponding, developing situation in time. The main diagram is divided into four sub-sections of which B and C represent the two pairs of sub-systems in the domestic economy. Section A carries the rate of interest determined by the inter-section of goods and money markets (*IE* and *LM* curves) to a function determining the volume of overseas funds (*F*) attracted to the United Kingdom. Only the positive part of this *F*-function is shown in section A, but the full function is shown in section A′, where this part of the diagram has been turned to match the incoming or outgoing funds with the current balance of payments.[3] The balance of payments itself is shown very much in the way illustrated earlier (Fig. 4.1) but with the import function (*M*) responding very rapidly to attempts to accelerate the rate of growth of the economy by increasing the level of aggregate demand. At the chosen point in time it is taken that there is no excess demand in the economy, but that wages and prices are rising rapidly because of their mutually interdependent responses to the internal pressures to equalise and improve rewards. It is assumed that wages have pulled ahead of prices to some extent and that real wages are a little above their equilibrium level and that employment is just a little below. If recent policies have been directed at restricting the level of demand in order to prevent a deterioration of the balance of pay-ments position, the slightly depressed position of output may be accounted for by firms' liquidity positions as well as by decisions to reduce output because of high wage costs. With employment only a little below the equi-librium level, high incomes from employment will be tending to push up consumption levels and this will exert pressure to raise aggregate demand above aggregate supply.

The control problem here, not unlike some situations in the earlier 1970s, would be seen as one requiring a continuous checking of aggregate

Fig. 10.2 A model for policy discussion

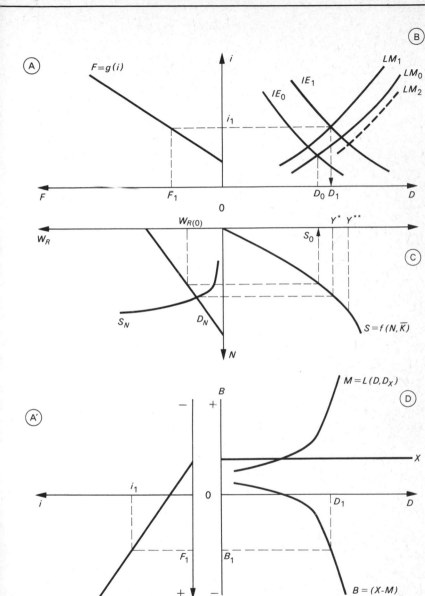

demand in order to keep both the balance of payments and the level of prices within bounds. The full problem of how to steer the economy back towards its growth path without these other two measures exceeding the limits set by policy seems, for long periods, to have been abandoned as incapable of solution. According to the theory of economic control, it should have been possible to have selected a level of demand that would have been adequate to ensure full employment and at the same time to have manipulated monetary conditions to produce an interest rate sufficiently high to attract funds from overseas. The target level of output and demand is shown at Y^* corresponding to D_1 and S_1; the possibility of it being set at a higher level to fulfil a more ambitious growth or employment target such as Y^{**} is not considered, although it may have formed an unrealised part of some earlier policy mixes. The interest rate produced is i_1 and, carried to the F-function and then down to sections A' and D of the diagram, this just covers the balance of payments deficit at B_1. It perhaps goes without saying that the more confidently such a policy is applied, the more the funds attracted are likely to remain in the United Kingdom. Vacillations in policy are bound to produce uncertainty and to encourage speculation.

A policy of this sort, whether wholly desirable on other grounds or not, becomes impossible if the extension of aggregate demand is followed by an unwanted and uncontrolled increase in the money supply. In the face of such unintended increases the measures required to bring back the monetary equilibrium curve from a position such as LM_2 to LM_1 as required for an intersection with IE_1 might necessitate very stringent measures of control so that business could find itself without funds to expand and perhaps without the confidence to do so. The excess demand, $(D_1 - S_0)$ assuming that there is little movement from the original supply position, would be mopped up by purchases of imported goods, which would begin to move the IE curve to the left again, and by rising prices. It is because of such difficulties that the secondary mix of objectives is accepted, but even this is not easily achieved if government expenditure cannot be controlled. The damage to the welfare objective which expenditure cuts entail invites a solution from the taxation side of the fiscal equation, but increases in personal taxation are politically dangerous and greater company taxation may inhibit the economy's ability to expand supply. The attractions of some other way of financing, or reducing, an excess of government spending are clear as is the contribution that a wealth tax might make.

The alternative approach, designed to achieve the secondary, suboptimal, set of objectives is one of intermittently suppressing aggregate demand by both fiscal and monetary policies, which can work together in these circumstances, and of imposing controls of one kind or another on incomes in order to contain the price and wage pressures which are bound to be generated. With floating exchange rates, it should have been possible to relax the attention paid to the balance of payments objective, but the rise in commodity prices and in the price of oil after the 1973 Middle East War have made it very difficult to do so. At this point the domestic economic system connects with yet another massive set of inter-related factors: the international monetary system. Some of the features of this system have become so fragile in recent years that it would be considered quite irresponsible to permit a really large fall in the value of a major currency.

10.5 Stability and rigidities in the control of economic systems
Economic policy is determined not only by a knowledge of what measures ought to be taken but by what is possible and practicable. Rigidities within the economic system place firm limits on the extent to which policy instruments can be used and also in the ways in which they are applied. In economic models, the manipulation of government expenditure seems difficult mainly in the decisions about the magnitude and the timing of the changes to be made but the practical decision is complicated by the size and nature of projects already in hand. Earlier decisions about the level of government spending cannot instantly be set aside; contracts will have been placed, some projects will be partially completed and the cancellation of others may affect the viability of long-term plans in vital sectors of the economy or in the wider life of the nation. The earlier years of the Labour Government which came to power in 1964 were marked by such a situation when expenditures appropriate to an annual growth rate of 4 per cent continued long after it became apparent that growth of this order would not be achieved. The natural momentum of public expenditure makes it a clumsy component of policy and the main burden of short-run variations in fiscal policy is, therefore, thrown on to changes in taxation. Here, too, sensitive manipulation is far from easy since some receipts, such as those from company taxation, depend on rates set in earlier periods and changes made, of course, will have effect in future periods when conditions may be quite different. A further aspect of taxation which must be taken into account is that the receipts from many kinds of taxes vary as the total of incomes and expenditure varies. A negative feedback is thus established to modify the effects of fiscal policy so that it works against deviations from target income levels. In principle, this exerts a powerful influence towards stability, but since not all economic events are subject to regulation, it can work against spontaneous but desired changes in the level of activity. The pattern of the relationship between income and taxation is illustrated in

Fig. 10.3   Taxation and stabilisation

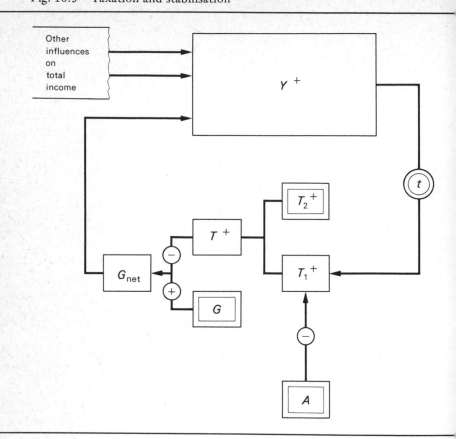

block diagram form in Fig. 10.3 and it will be noticed that money values rather than price-corrected ones are used here. The fact that the operation of 'automatic stabilisation' is through money values and not through their real equivalents is likely to produce some side effects. The most obvious of these is that the real value of tax allowances, marked A in the diagram, tends to be eroded in real terms during periods of rising prices. This can be compensated for by making adjustments to the system of tax allowances, but in the meantime increased tax payments will be likely to have given rise to higher wage demands and to have encouraged an acceleration in the wage—price interactions.

The indications that the economic system does contain at least one stabilising device which appears to work moderately well adds a little force to the arguments of those who recommend policies of minimum intervention. The theoretical basis for such policies rests partly on monetary theories of income determination and partly on models of stabilisation about an equilibrium position or, dynamically, about an equilibrium growth path.[4] It does not follow that policies which are suitable for an economy which is experiencing minor deviations from an established growth path are appropriate for one which has been far from its equilibrium path for a long time.

If British policy in the later 1960s is considered in the light of whether or not tax changes exerted a stabilising influence on the economy with respect to its growth path, the probable conclusion must be that they did not. The statistical evidence is not altogether clear[5] but as this was a time during which the growth objective was being discarded and the sub-optimal objectives of reasonably full employment and an improved balance of payments were becoming accepted as of primary importance, this is not surprising. The intention of policy was to frustrate expansion in order to secure more immediate objectives on which economic survival appeared to depend.

Notes and references

1. See W. Ross Ashby, *An Introduction to Cybernetics*, Chapman and Hall, 1956, especially Ch. 11.

2. See R. G. D. Allen, *Macro-economic theory*, Macmillan, 1967, Ch. 18, especially 18.3, pp. 350–2.

3. The concepts of section A in the diagram were suggested by H. G. Johnson's article 'Theoretical problems of the international monetary system', *Pakistan Development Review* (reprinted in *International Finance: Selected Readings*, ed. R. N. Cooper).

4. An early but full statement is given by Milton Friedman in 'A monetary and fiscal framework for economic stability', *American Economic Review*, 1948.

5. M. Artis writing on 'Fiscal policy for stabilisation' in *The Labour Government's Economic Record, 1964–1970*, 1972, ed. Beckerman, reports statistical tests and draws the inference that tax policy was somewhat destabilising during the period reviewed.

11
A final comment

The approach to macro-economic analysis which has been put forward contains few innovations but brings together some influences which have become very well recognised in recent years. Five sets of ideas have seemed to be relevant. These are:

1. The equivalence of the structure of standard Keynesian and general equilibrium models in the absence of very special assumptions.
2. The shifting of the ground of the debate towards processes of adjustment within a system in which constrained decisions in disequilibrium and the information flows which they generate are significant.
3. The acceptance of an equilibrium growth path as a long-period datum to which short-run positions may be related.
4. The importance of expectations in economic decision making. This both follows directly from Keynes and is in line with much modern work in economics and econometrics.
5. The requirements for control that follow from the recognition that economic policy is concerned with the regulation of a complex open system.
6. The recognition that the openness of the economic system extends to social change.

In many ways the view of the economy which emerges is very much a Keynesian one, but the introduction of, in effect, a learning process by means of which expectations and plans are both unchanged when deviations are small but extensively revised when changes are large or frequently repeated makes some revision necessary. Where revisions have been made to established analyses they are presented tentatively and not without a proper humility, but it does seem that events both in the field of economic analysis and in the real and observable world now demand some systematic presentation at a fairly fundamental level. The approach through which this has been attempted is one that provides a framework for discussion rather than one which will provide neat answers. This, it is suggested, is as it should be, for there are real points of difference involved. In two respects, the view presented is an incomplete one. The employment of a one-commodity model is not fully defensible in terms of economic theory, but it is so on the grounds of clarity of exposition and of direct relationship to policy issues. The other respect in which the approach is insufficiently detailed concerns the treatment of financial markets and the institutions through which their workings are expressed. These are matters of central importance and yet they are often dealt with rather summarily in economic analysis, being hived off as topics of specialist concern. One point of contact between macro-economic models and these financial processes is through 'flow of funds' analysis. This is a potentially powerful technique which has begun to yield new insights and has made a contribution the views on economic control put forward by the Cambridge economists and mentioned briefly in an earlier chapter. Many difficulties remain to be overcome before the two approaches can be reconciled, but it has been suggested that flow of funds analysis might have a special role to play in the study of the adjustment processes which have been our main concern.

Appendix I   A technical commentary

AI.1 Static and dynamic analysis in economics

A further word is needed concerning the legitimacy of applying comparative static diagrams in the analysis of situations in which the dynamic adjustment towards a new equilibrium is known to be the most important feature. There are many advantages in using static models in this way; they are much more easily understood than the corresponding mathematical analysis and they allow the consideration of alternative and related situations without redrafting and solving a new set of differential or difference equations. Often, too, they give a more ready intuitive 'feel' for a problem. Comparative static analysis however may give only a limited understanding of the nature of the full solution of the underlying dynamic model or of the way in which the solution is likely to change if lags are introduced or if the values of coefficients are altered. The relationship between a comparative-static analysis and the dynamic process which it illustrates is a precise one. When static models are used to show a stage in a dynamic process, the diagrams display some steady, or stationary, state which the corresponding dynamic model will reach as the economic forces involved play themselves out. It is in this sense that the Samuelson correspondence principle should be interpreted. The fact that comparative static diagrams show stationary solutions of dynamic models does not mean that they cannot be applied in evolving situations nor that the analysis must be confined to a comparison of equilibrium conditions. The characteristics of the functions represented in the diagrams can be changed as can the values of the variables entering into them and alternative steady states of the dynamic process can be considered, including the effects of departures from equilibrium and of entries into the process from non-equilibrium initial positions. Examples of this latter type of application are the analyses of approaches to equilibrium from situations of excess demand, or excess price, in market models and of sequences such as those involved in the cobweb models.

The diagrammatic approach employed in Chapters 7 to 10 is not very different in kind from other comparative static analyses. Each of the sub-systems, monetary, expenditure, employment and production, consists of a set of relationships representing economic forces which operate to produce an equilibrium in the sector concerned. By separating the sub-systems operating primarily on aggregate demand from those which act mainly on aggregate supply, the alternative possibilities of equilibrium can be indicated. Full equilibrium is not attainable, of course, unless the equilibria established in all of the sub-systems are compatible. The device of splitting the horizontal axis between the two sets of influences allows a pause for considering which of the adjustment processes is likely to follow when the sub-system equilibria are not compatible with each other at the ruling price level. The necessity of choosing between alternative equilibrating processes is not a new thing in economics and is familiar in ordinary single-market disequilibrium where either Marshallian or Walrasian processes may predominate. In macro-economic situations, the alternative methods of adjustment towards equilibrium are even less likely to give equivalent results than in micro-economics.

Another point of reconciliation between static and dynamic equilibrium concepts needs to be considered. Acceptance of the idea of equilibrium along a growth path involves rather different concepts from those with which short-period adjustment models are concerned. The maintenance of an equilibrium position along a time-path carries an implication of constant and instantaneous adjustment. The application of short-period models to positions along the growth path is likely to be concerned with delayed and imperfect adjustments and so requires a suspension of the assumption of perfect adjustment. We are using models to attempt an ordering of ideas and short of an ideal state of total understanding we cannot expect complete consistency between models used for different purposes. As a working method, we could take a short period of time and regard the growth path rates of production and income as sufficiently unchanging to permit their use as data during the short time with which the analysis is concerned. This, naturally, implies their use as points of reference, not their equivalence to actual values either as observed or as indicated by the working of the model. The distinction between the assumptions required for long- and for short-run equilibrium are perhaps less critical if a neo-classical view is taken to be appropriate for long-run adjustment, regardless of the short run view.

AI.2 The use of simultaneous equation models

The use of systems of equations has been avoided in the main text but there may be some advantage in setting out the Keynesian and Classical models in this form, both for comparison and to indicate the merits and limitations of this method of presentation. A very common way of displaying the basic *IS–LM* model is in the form of six equations:

(1) A consumption function

$$\frac{C}{P} = f\left(\frac{Y}{P}\right)$$

(2) An investment function

$$\frac{I}{P} = g(r)$$

(3) An equilibrium condition

$$\frac{Y}{P} = \frac{C + I}{P}$$

Equations [I.1] to [I.3]

(4) A money demand function

$$\frac{M_D}{P} = h\left(r, \frac{Y}{P}\right)$$

(5) A money supply condition

$$M_S = \overline{M}_S$$

(6) An equilibrium condition

$$M_D = M_S$$

Equations [I.4] to [I.6]

Equations [I.1] to [I.3] give the *IS* curve and [I.4] to [I.6] provide the *LM* curve. The symbols have the usual meanings, but values are in money, not constant price terms, that is:

C = consumption in money terms;
I = investment in money terms;
Y = money income;
P = price level;
r = interest rate;
M_D = demand for money;
M_S = supply of money.

The symbols f, g, h and, below, ϕ_1 and ϕ_2 are functional signs of the kind used earlier although not necessarily attached to the same relationships.

If the equation for the real wage as determined by the marginal productivity of labour is added, we have

$$\frac{W}{P} = \frac{dQ}{dN} = \phi_1'(N) \tag{I.7}$$

Here, Q is the volume of output, dQ/dN represents the rate of change of output with respect to N, the labour employed, and ϕ_1' indicates the first derivative of the production function. With the quantity of money (M_S) determined outside the system, either the money wage or the price level (P) can be given a value independently. If the price level is taken to be fixed, then the system of equations can be solved to provide values for the remaining six variables (Y, W, r, C, I, N).

It has been pointed out by a number of writers that systems such as that outlined can be restated in market form with only small changes. All that is required is to set up a labour market by adding a labour supply function:

$$N_S = \phi_2\left(\frac{W}{P}\right) \tag{I.8}$$

and an equilibrium condition

$$N_D = N_S \tag{I.9}$$

Equation [1.7], or more strictly its inverse, provides the demand function and, integrated, it gives the production function:

$$Q = \phi_1(N) \tag{I.10}$$

Equations [I.1] and [I.2] together form a simple aggregate demand function and aggregate supply is given by equation [I.10]. The real income variable, Y/P, in equations [I.1] and [I.4] refers to expected income, since these are demand functions which represent conditional schedules showing what the outcome *would* be *if* a particular set of conditions were fulfilled.

The relationship of both models to the analysis developed in this book can be seen very readily as can the restricted amount of discussion which these models permit. It is of interest to note that working with equations only slightly different from [I.1] to [I.6], Milton Friedman has drawn the distinction between Keynesian income—expenditure theory and the quantity theory as being dependent on whether the price level or real income is held constant, the solution of the equation system being contingent on which of the two conditions is embodied in a final, seventh, equation.

AI.3 Block diagrams and mathematical analysis

The block diagrams used in the discussion of adjustment sequences can be related both to the equation systems discussed above and to dynamic adjustment processes. Taken at face value, each relationship in the block diagram can be listed to give an equation system rather like the market system of the previous section, but with some values held constant at non-equilibrium values other systems would result. Alternatively, fixed values could be allocated and the direction of causation reversed or, again, lags could be introduced and yet other systems developed. Provided that strict conventions are established and adhered to, direct translation into mathematical form is possible.

The diagrams as shown in the text are rather simplified versions of the control diagrams introduced into economic analysis by A. W. Phillips and others. As we have used them primarily to give a foundation for discussion, the conventions have not been followed with absolute strictness when clarity required a less constrained approach, but the method of conversion into equations can easily be shown. Since the block diagrams are most useful in dynamic analysis, the growth model which was discussed in section 8.3 and which is dealt with again in note AI.4 is used as an illustration.

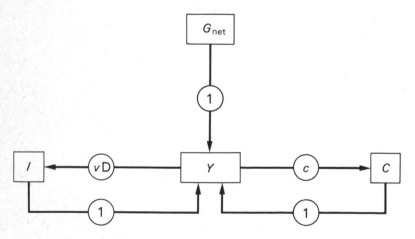

In the diagram above, D is the differential operator, d/dt, and the other symbols have the usual meanings, G_N being the autonomously determined net effect of fiscal policy. As before the direct arrows indicate addition and the constant relationship between the elements has been indicated even when it is unity. The system therefore reads

$Y = C + I + G_N$ (The three arrows connecting to Y)

$$I = v \frac{dY}{dt} \qquad \text{(The left-hand branch)}$$

$$C = cY \qquad \text{(The right-hand branch)}$$

If it is felt that the reaction of investment expenditures to increases in income is likely to be delayed, a lag can be inserted using the following convention:

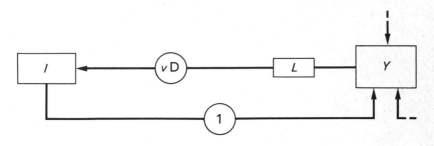

The model which results depends on the form of the lag chosen. Further discussion of the use of block diagrams and of additional conventions designed to give greater precision can be found in the references given at the end of this note.

AI.4 Equilibrium growth paths
A fairly detailed outline of the simple growth models and the assumptions on which they are based was given in Chapter 8, but a more thorough explanation of the way in which the growth path formulae are derived is needed. Some indications of the basic relationships have been given in the discussion of block diagrams and the fundamental assumption of instantaneous adjustment to the equilibrium condition along the path have already been mentioned. The relevant conditions in the Harrod–Domar models is that the equality of saving with planned investment should hold along the growth path and there is also the assumption that aggregate supply and aggregate demand are in perfect adjustment, the volume of goods and services available being determined by the output/capital ratio. With investment depending on the rate of growth of output with respect to time so that

$$I = v \frac{dY}{dt} \qquad\qquad\qquad [I.11]$$

and with saving a constant proportion of income:

$$S = sY \qquad\qquad\qquad [I.12]$$

the equilibrium condition is satisfied when

$$sY = v \frac{dY}{dt} \qquad [\text{I}.13]$$

If this equation is rearranged and both sides are integrated, we have

$$\int \frac{s}{v} \, dt = \int \frac{1}{Y} \, dY \qquad [\text{I}.14]$$

from which, omitting the constants of integration,

$$\log_e Y = \frac{s}{v} t \qquad [\text{I}.15]$$

With the constants inserted and taken to the right-hand side, this produces

$$Y = Y_0 e^{(s/v)t} \qquad [\text{I}.16]$$

Here Y_0 is the level of output and income when $t = 0$, that is at the start of the growth process.

It is not appropriate to do more than indicate the general direction of the analysis. The growth path required to give a 'golden age' in which there is full employment as well as steady growth is one in which the labour force is growing at the same rate as output and productive capacity. The growth of the labour force is given by

$$N = N_0 e^{nt} \qquad [\text{I}.17]$$

and the equation of the growth rates of income and the labour force with an allowance made for the growth of labour productivity produces the conditions given in Chapter 8, equation [8.2].

It can be shown without difficulty that the rate of investment required by the equilibrium growth path produces an increase in the capital stock at the same exponential rate. This means that the proportion of capital to labour in the production process is unchanging and that the classical adjustment of the labour/capital ratio in response to changing factor prices is ruled out. The response to this in the Solow model referred to in Chapter 8 is to let total output be a function of the capital and labour employed without restriction:

$$Y = \phi(K, N) \qquad [\text{I}.18]$$

Maintaining the saving-investment equilibrium condition, the rate of change of capital stock with respect to time must be

$$\frac{dK}{dt} = I = sY \qquad [\text{I}.19]$$

Building the labour availability given by [I.17] into the production function [I.18] now gives

$$\frac{dK}{dt} = sY = s \cdot \phi(K, N_0 e^{nt}) \tag{I.20}$$

This gives the rate at which the capital stock should grow in order to keep the labour force fully employed even when the growth path is not the one 'warranted' by the Harrod model. The further conclusions are to be found in Solow's article.

References

The Friedman model is set out in 'A monetary theory of nominal income' in *Monetary Theory and Monetary Policy in the 1970s*, eds G. Clayton, J. C. Gilbert and R. Sedgwick, Oxford University Press, 1971. A key work in the exposition of economic control theory is *An Introduction to Economic Cybernetics* by Oskar Lange, Pergamon, 1970, and a brief summary of the application of control diagrams and their associated equations is given in Chapter 9 of R. G. D. Allen's *Mathematical Economics* (Macmillan, 1965) and in Chapter 5 of the same author's *Macro-Economic Theory* (Macmillan, 1967). The Solow model of economic growth is to be found in 'A contribution to the theory of economic growth', *Quarterly Journal of Economics*, vol. 70, 1956.

Appendix II   Selected statistics of the UK economy, 1951–72

Year	Gross Domestic Product	Growth path of GDP at 2.8% p.a.	Exports	Imports	Unemployment percentage	Wage rate 1963 = 100	Retail prices 1963 = 100	Interest rate
1951	25.86	25.70	5.37	5.24	1.2	59.4	67	3.78
1952	25.87	26.42	5.26	4.85	2.1	64.3	73	4.23
1953	27.08	27.16	5.48	5.23	1.8	67.1	75	4.08
1954	28.07	27.92	5.78	5.42	1.5	69.9	76	3.75
1955	29.04	28.70	6.14	5.97	1.2	74.5	80	4.17
1956	29.59	29.50	6.41	5.99	1.3	80.1	83.8	4.73
1957	30.17	30.33	6.57	6.14	1.6	84.0	86.9	4.98
1958	30.10	31.18	6.47	6.20	2.2	86.7	89.5	4.98
1959	31.14	32.05	6.64	6.61	2.3	89.0	90.1	4.82
1960	32.60	32.95	7.01	7.40	1.7	90.9	91.0	5.42
1961	33.76	33.88	7.22	7.35	1.6	94.6	94.1	6.20
1962	34.06	34.82	7.34	7.49	2.1	97.2	98.0	5.98
1963	35.45	35.80	7.65	7.76	2.6	100.0	100.0	5.58
1964	37.50	36.80	7.95	8.48	1.7	104.6	103.2	6.03
1965	38.47	37.83	8.34	8.56	1.5	108.3	108.1	6.42
1966	39.22	38.88	8.68	8.78	1.6	113.1	112.4	6.80
1967	40.12	39.99	8.78	9.37	2.5	117.6	115.2	6.69
1968	41.64	41.10	9.81	10.05	2.5	126.6	120.6	7.39
1969	42.16	42.25	10.72	10.35	2.7	133.8	127.2	8.88
1970	42.79	43.43	11.25	10.87	2.6	146.5	135.3	9.16
1971	43.67	44.65	12.06	11.40	3.4	163.2	148.0	9.07
1972	44.34	45.90	12.43	12.55	3.8	185.2	158.5	9.11

Sources: National Income and Expenditure Blue Book, Monthly Digest of Statistics, Central Statistical Office.
The British Economy: Key Statistics, 1900–70. Published by The Times Newspapers Ltd for London and Cambridge Economic Service.

Note: Wage rates refer to male workers in manufacturing industry; interest rates are the flat yields on 2½ per cent Consols. Values are at 1970 prices in £thousand millions.

Index

Note: Figures in *italic* refer to the **Notes and references** at the end of each chapter.

Acceleration principle, 70
Advertising, 17, 18
Aggregate demand, 6, 36, 41, 54,
    55, 57, 63, 68, 80, 83, 85, 88,
    92, 98, 106, 113, 115
Aggregate supply, 54, 55, 57, 63,
    85, 91, 98, 113, 115
Aggregation, 21–9, 41, 49
Allen, R. G. D., *109, 119*
Artis, M., *109*
Ashby, W. Ross, *109*
Aspiration level, 73, 80, 83, 91, 92

Balance of payments, 33 (dia.), 34,
    86–90, 102, 104, 106, 107,
    109
Bank rate, 2
Baumol, W. J., *20*
Block diagrams, 59, 63, 68, 72,
    116–17
Bond market, 26, 27, 38, 41
Burman, J. P., *79*

Cambridge
    economists, 19, 84, 89, 110
    view of economic control, 89,
    111

Capital
    formation, *90*
    cost of, 69
    goods, 49
    stock, 19, 70, 81, 118, 119
    working, 62
Capital-output ratio, 83, 84, 117
Classical system, 6, 8–9, 12, 20, 35,
    36, 45, 51, 53, 63, 68, 69, 74,
    75, 98
Clower, R. W., 10, 43, 44–8, *50*
Command economy, 12
Computable models, 76, 77
Consumption
    expenditures, 4, 18, 57, 60, 61,
    67, 68, 114
    hypotheses, 45, 69, 70, 99
    and income, 5, 45, 69
Control, economic, 98–109
Correspondence principle, 64, 112

D.C.E., *10*
Decision process, 53, 64, 103
Demand, 23–5, 54, 57, 67, 78, 106
    curve, 15, 43, 45
    excess, *see* Excess Demand
Depression, economic, 66–9

Devaluation, 87, 89
Devletoglou, N. E., *65*
Dimsdale, N. H., and Glyn, A. J., *65*
Disequilibrium, 28, 41, 51—65, 69
Domar, E., 83, *90*
Dual-decision hypothesis, 44, 45
Dynamic processes, 45, 103,
    112—13, 116—17

Economic models, 1—10
Eisner, R., *20, 65*
Employment, 6, 54, 57, 61, 72, 79,
    81, 90, 102, 104
Equation systems, 21—4, *65*, 114
Equations of exchange, 21—5
Equilibrium, 12, 22—7, 28, 38, 39,
    41—5, 53, 57, 69, 80, 81, 98
  general, *see* General Equilibrium
  growth path, 80, 83, 84, 86, 99,
    103—4, 117—19
  market, 12—18, 25, 47
  stability of, 13, 28, *29*
Excess demand, 13, 25, 26, 41—4,
    52, 55, 57, 62, 71, 72, 76, 81,
    88, 104, 106
Excess demand curve, 13, 14 (dia.),
    24
Excess supply, 13, 15, 25, 41, 42,
    52, 55, 61, 62, 88
Exchange economy, 21, 22—5, 29
Exchange rates, 88, 89, 107
Expectations, 6, 7, 44, 45, 47, 54,
    55, 68, 73, 99
Exports, 34, 86—9

Feedback, 4, 13, 60, 107
Feldstein, M. S., and Fleming, J. S.,
    39
Fiscal policy, 74, 89, 90, 106, 107
Flow of funds analysis, 111
Free goods, 24
Friedman, M., 46, 69, 78, 79, 99,
    109, 115, *119*

Galbraith, J. K., 17, 18, *20*
G.D.P., 66, 86, 99

General equilibrium, 21—9, 38, 52,
    97, 110
General Theory, 3, 4, 6, 30, 31, 44,
    48, 74
Government expenditure, 4, 7, 9,
    34, 54, 57
Growth
  economic, 80—90
  Harrod—Domar model, 83,
    117—18
  Solow model, 118—19
Growth path, 83, 87 (dia.), 98,
    103—4, 113, 117—19
Growth rate
  natural, 84
  warranted, 84, 119

Hansen, A., 32, *39, 40*
Harrod, R., 83, *90*
Hicks, J. R., *20*, 32, 36, *39*, 43, 47
Hines, A. G., 37, *40*
  and Catephores, G., *39*, 50
Hypotheses, in economic science,
    77—9

I.M.F., 8
Imports, 34, 85, 86—9, 104
Income, 4, 6, 7, 9, 31, 54, 69, 78,
    92
  determination, 4—7, 30—5
  disposable, 10
Income effects on stability of
    equilibrium, 17, *20*, 43, 44,
    50
Income—expenditure model, 30—7,
    48
Incomes
  factor, 54
  policy, 93—6
Income-constrained decisions, 46,
    54, 66, 67, 98
Inflation, 36, 37, 71—6, 91, 96
Information flows, 13—17, 19, 28,
    46—9, 53, 80, 92, 93, 110
Injections—withdrawals model, 33,
    34

Instruments, policy, 79, 90, 101, 102, 103
Interest rates, 2, 3, 6, 9, 19, 30, 31, 32, 50, 60, 68, 79, 90, 106, 114
Investment, 3, 4, 8, 9, 11, 31, 49, 54, 57, 62, 67, 68, 81−3, 114, 116−17
  interest inelasticity of, 3, 6, 32
IS−LM model, 32, 33 (dia.), 36, 37, 48, 62, 63, 71

Jackson, D., and Turner, H. A., 97
Johnson, H. G., 109
Johnston, R. E., 97
Jones, A., 91, 92, 97
Jorgenson, D. W., 40
Junankar, P. N., 79

Kaldor, N., 89
Keynes, J. M., 2, 5, 6, 7, 12, 30, 31, 36, 37, 44, 49, 66, 74, 76, 110
Keynesian models, 2−8, 10, 27, 28, 29, 30−7, 41, 48, 51, 53, 67, 68−9, 71, 72, 75, 80, 91, 98, 102, 110, 114
Kuhn, T. S., 78

Labour
  demand, 57, 58 (dia.), 59, 81, 82 (dia.), 115
  market, 27, 42, 59, 60, 63, 72, 93−6
  supply, 43, 57, 59−61, 68, 71, 72, 93−6
Labour Government, 2, 94, 107
Lags, 13, 70, 75, 112
Lange, O., 119
Leijonhufvud, A., 10, 13, 30, 46, 47, 48, 49, 54
Lipsey, R. G.
  and Archibald, G. C., 43, 50
  and Parkin, M., 94
Liquidity, 51, 55, 98
  preference, 30, 32, 78
  trap, 32, 33 (dia.), 36

Marginal
  efficiency of capital, 30, 32
  productivity, 60, 72, 81, 115
  propensity to consume, 8, 59, 83
Market, 9, 21, 22, 27
  labour, see Labour Market
  boundaries, 18
  structure of models, 27, 41, 48
  system, 11−19, 29, 45
Marris, R., 20
Marshall, A., 12
Mill, J. S., 12, 29
Monetary policy, 5, 7, 54, 74, 90, 106
Money, 26, 75
  demand for, 6, 7, 9, 26, 31, 57, 58, 78, 114
  illusion, 79
  market, 9, 27
  quantity theory of, 78
  supply, 6, 7, 9, 32, 34, 35, 36, 54, 57, 60, 74, 75, 93, 106, 114, 115
Monopoly power, 17, 18, 37, 75
Multiplier, 5, 46, 67, 89, 90
  balanced budget, 10

Neo-classical
  economics, 20, 37, 38, 97, 102
  models, 14, 19, 20, 39, 84, 98
Nield, R., 89
Numéraire, 22, 23, 25

'Oxford Economists', 3
Objectives of economic policy, 102−7

Parkin, M., 94
Patinkin, D., 26, 29, 75
Permanent income hypothesis, 45, 69, 99
Phillips, A. W., 94, 119
Phillips curve, 94, 95
Pigou, A. C., 12
Population, working, 81, 84, 85, 86

Price, 13, 19, 36, 46, 51, 58, 63, 72, 93
  determination, 13—17, 21—4
  discrepancy curve, 13
  flexibility, 36, 68, 80
  level, 8, 43, 48, 57, 60, 104, 114
  as signal, 46, 47, 62, 68
Prices, 35, 36, 48—9, 52, 66, 68, 71, 74, 88, 91—7
  distribution of, 15, 16, 18, 46
Production function, 9, 19, 53, 60, 62, 63, 72, 73, 81, 115
Productivity, 81—2, 84, 86, 92, 93
Profit, 17, 20, 55, 69, 85
  maximisation, 13, 17, 68, 72, 73, 85
  motive 15, 17, 74

Radcliffe report, 93
Real-balance effect, 26, 43
Recession, 61—3, 70, 99
Re-switching, 19
Ricardo, D., 12
Robinson, Joan, *20*

Sales-revenue maximisation, 72
Samuelson, P. A., *65*, 112
Saving, 4, 8, 9, 30, 31, 34, 49, 89, 117
Say, J. B., 25
Search process, 15—17, 16 (dia.), 45, 46—7
Smith, A., 12
Social factors, 71, 91, 96, 97, 99, 100, 110
Solow, R. M., *119*
Solow growth model, *see* Growth, Solow model

Stabilisation, 107—9
Stagflation, 37
Stigler, G., 15, *20*, 46
Stocks, 67, 69
System
  economy as, 54—61, 99—102

Targets, policy, 101, 106
Tâtonnement, 28, 39, 47
Taxation, 4, 8, 9, 10, 34, 54, 57, 59, 104, 106, 107, 108
Technical progress, *97*
Technological change, 49, 81, 93
Telser, L. S., 46, *50*
Trade unions, 36, 42, 43, 73, 75—6, 91, 92, 93, 94, 96, 100
Treasury Bills, 103

Uncertainty, 17, 53, 99, 106
Unemployment, 8, 28, 35, 41, 42, 45, 49, 66, 72, 79, 89, 91, 92, 95, 96, *97*
Utility, 44

Variety, Law of Requisite, 101
Variety in system, 99
Velocity of circulation, 75, 93

Wage
  rates, 8, 57, 93—5
  real, 8, 53, 55, 57, 59, 61, 62, 67, 68, 72, 75, 115
  rigidity, 43, 49
Wage-bargaining, 96
Wages, 104
Walras, L., 28
Walras's Law, 26, 45
Welfare, 102, 103, 106